Shades of the Old, Wild West

Papoose of Indian babies — many were killed during the extermination period and western expansion.

(From: *Little Journeys to Alaska and Canada*, Marion M. George, A. Flanagan Company, Chicago, Illinois, 1901.)

SHADES OF THE OLD, WILD WEST

Rex T. Jackson

HERITAGE BOOKS
2019

HERITAGE BOOKS
AN IMPRINT OF HERITAGE BOOKS, INC.

Books, CDs, and more—Worldwide

For our listing of thousands of titles see our website
at
www.HeritageBooks.com

Published 2019 by
HERITAGE BOOKS, INC.
Publishing Division
5810 Ruatan Street
Berwyn Heights, Md. 20740

Copyright © 2019 Rex T. Jackson

Cover illustration by Maynard Dixon from
Clarence E. Mulford's *Hopalong Cassidy*, A. L. Burt Company, New York, 1910.
Original illustrations by the author.

All rights reserved. No part of this book may be reproduced or transmitted in any form or by any means, electronic or mechanical, including photocopying, recording or by any information storage and retrieval system without written permission from the author, except for the inclusion of brief quotations in a review.

International Standard Book Numbers
Paperbound: 978-0-7884-5867-5

Shades of the Old, Wild West

Contents

ix...Introduction

1...Scalper James Kirker: Genocide and Western Expansion
9...Joaquin Murietta: Robin Hood of El Dorado
17...William Tilghman: Legendary Lawman
29...Pinkertons, Gads Hill, and the Showdown-Shootout at Roscoe
41...Life and Times of Belle Starr
51...The Bloody Benders: Evil Along the Osage Trail
59...Calamity Jane: Teamster, Showgirl, Prostitute and Nurse
67...Tombstone: Thirty Seconds at the O.K. Corral
79...Chief Black Kettle and the Slaughters at Sand Creek and Washita
89...The Long Walk and the Navajo Exodus
95...Pacific Railroad Disaster: Engine of Western Conquest
105...Steamboat A-Comin'
121...The Dalton Gang's Last Stand: Riding the Razor's Edge
131...Minnesota the Beautiful and the Botched Mass Hanging
139...Goodnight-Loving Trail: The Life and Times of Goodnight, Loving, and Adair
145...John Wesley Hardin: A Homicidal Desperado
153...Henry Starr: Robber with Distinction

161...Additional Illustrations
173...Index
183...About the Author

Introduction

THE TAMING of America's Wild West was an ongoing process that involved bloody wars, hardships, new technologies, law enforcement and much more. Many of the players became famous and infamous, with some using their minds and backs during this rough and rugged era while others resorted to the gun to get what they wanted. The conquering of the West is a quagmire of historical importance, offering a source of national pride and also shame and disgrace. One such individual that helped to make the West wild was "Billy the Kid."

William Henry (Billy the Kid) McCarty Jr. was born in New York City, New York, on September 17, 1859, to Irish parents, Patrick Henry McCarty and Catherine Devine McCarty. Patrick died while Billy was still very young and his mother eventually traveled out West and settled in Wichita, Kansas; and a short time later she relocated again to Silver City, New Mexico Territory, where she met and married a man named William Antrim. During Billy's lifetime he would use several names, like William Henry Bonney, Kid Antrim—and, of course, Billy the Kid.

Billy's childhood was a difficult one and his stepfather did little to help the situation. As a result, he was always in and out of hot water: at the tender age of twelve he had already stabbed a man to death; and by the age of eighteen, he was known as a horse thief who had reportedly killed at least twenty-one men—including a hired gun sent out to assassinate him.

Billy eventually met John H. Tunstall who became like a father-figure to him, but it didn't last long. On February 18, 1878, during the Lincoln County Range War, Tunstall was gunned down by Billy Morton and Jesse Evans. Billy was devastated and set out to even the score—he did, at a place called Dead Man's Hole located between Lincoln and Roswell.

To bring the "Kid" to justice, Sheriff Patrick ("Pat") Garrett was called in to do the job; Garrett was an acquaintance of Billy but was a sworn peace officer with the task of apprehending the outlaw. By December 23, 1880, Sheriff Garrett had corralled Billy at an old deserted stone cabin at a place called Stinking Springs on Taiban Creek and taken him into custody. Back in Lincoln, Billy, not keen at the prospect of dangling at the end of a hemp rope, decided it was high time to make his escape. On April 28, 1881, finding his opportunity, he managed to get his hands on a gun and kill his guard, J.W. Bell. He also shot another guard, Robert W. Ollinger, who was on his way back from a café across the street; Billy shot him in the face from an upstairs window looking out on the street below. Afterwards, Billy made good on his escape and left the waiting noose in the dust.

Once again Pat Garrett was put on the trail of Billy the Kid. For over two months Garrett searched high and low for his elusive quarry, until the night of July 14-15, 1881; Garrett had tracked Billy to the Pete Maxwell Ranch located near Fort Sumner. After ascertaining that the desperado was not there, he waited inside the house in a dark bedroom. Just after the stroke of midnight Billy arrived and sauntered into the house, but after noticing a couple of Garrett's deputies lurking around outside, he backed into the bedroom where Garrett was waiting for him. Billy reportedly asked: "Quien es?"—meaning: "Who is it?" Garrett, recognizing his voice fired two shots—one of the rounds landed in his twenty-one year old chest. Billy the Kid fell to the floor dead, a victim of a .45 caliber slug from Garrett's Colt revolver; Billy's lifeless corpse was still clutching his own weapon tightly. There was no big to-do: Billy the Kid was buried that very night in the local cemetery; however, the legend of Billy the Kid lived on in books, magazines, television, and movies.

When Captain Meriwether Lewis and Captain William Clark headed out on their Corps of Discovery into the Far Western country of the Louisiana Purchase to the West Coast from St. Louis, Missouri, and the Mississippi River, the round trip took them two and one-half years to accomplish; however, after the Northern Pacific finished their second line to the Pacific Northwest from St. Paul, Minnesota, to Portland, Oregon, in September 1883, the trip by train only took nine days. The railroads played an important part in helping to claim the vastness of the American West. The second line to the West Coast took nineteen years to complete, through unforgiving terrain across 1,222 miles. When the track was laid through the Rocky Mountains, it was necessary to dig a 3,850-foot tunnel through solid granite; as well as a trestle bridge that was 1,800 feet in length. It was 130 miles of painstaking labor and difficulties to make it through the "Rockies." Most of the work was accomplished by a total of 25,000 Chinese laborers from the West Coast and Irish and Swedish workers laboring from the East. The final spike was driven in at Gold Creek, Montana, on September 8, connecting the two lines together.

And, who could forget Butch Cassidy and Harry Longabaugh (or the "Sundance Kid")? Known as the "Wild Bunch," their gang terrorized the West in the latter part of the 1800s. One of their robberies occurred on June 12, 1899 in Wyoming, where they made off with about $60,000. They stopped a Union Pacific train near Wilcox Station and robbed the express car. A deputy sheriff and a cowboy posse were organized to round up the gang, who were thought to be holed up at or near the hamlets of Dirty Devil Creek or Robbers' Roost Mesa.

Butch Cassidy and the Sundance Kid robbed trains and banks in Idaho, Utah, New Mexico, Nevada, Texas, and Montana. They eventually bought a huge acreage in Cholila, Chubut Province, Argentina, South America and tried to go "straight", but crime and the easy life beckoned to them once more. In 1908 they held up a silver mine courier near San Vicente, Bolivia, and a posse tracked them down and killed them in a blazing hailstorm of lead.

Many well-known legends of the Wild West had ties to other lesser-known individuals who piggybacked on their fame to some degree, and useful lessons can be gleaned from their stories as well. One of those who fits into this category is "Johnny" Ringo.

John Peters Ringo was born in Green Fork, Indiana, on May 3, 1850, to Martin and Mary Ringo. When John was about six-years-old the family moved to Missouri where he attended elementary school in Gallatin; reportedly, he also went to William Jewell College in Liberty, Missouri, to further his education. Ironically, the father of Frank and Jesse James, Robert James, who lived in Clay County near Kearny and was the pastor of the New Hope Baptist Church, helped to found William Jewell College and was one of the school's first board of trustees members; James was also instrumental in organizing and establishing other Christian congregations in the area.

During the American Civil War (1861-1865) life for the Ringo family became so dangerous and difficult in Missouri that they decided to skedaddle and move further west—but, en route to their promised land Martin accidentally shot himself in a freak mishap and was killed. The Ringo family pulled themselves together and continued on after the tragic incident until they reached San Jose, California, which is just south of San Francisco, and settled down.

In the late 1860s, Ringo left the nest and roamed and gallivanted about the Southwest where he, reportedly, met and kept company with the infamous John Wesley Hardin, who was, ironically, named after John Wesley the founder of Methodism. By the late 1870s, though, he had made his way to Tombstone, Arizona, and made friends with local outlaws and cattle rustlers—the Clantons and McLaurys of the O.K. Corral fame. However, after the death of Old Man Clanton who was killed in Guadalupe Canyon, Johnny Ringo was promoted to the head-of-the-class as chief cattle rustler. Along with William "Curly Bill" Brocious they formed a group that was later dubbed "The Cowboys," who boldly defied the law in Tombstone—mainly, Wyatt, Virgil, and Morgan Earp.

Ringo's Cowboys were ruthless enough to gain the attention of President Chester Alan Arthur, and on April 26, 1882, the president ordered regular army troops to be deployed to Arizona Territory to quell the outlaw uprising of theft and murder. The daring desperadoes had expanded their outlawry into Mexico, and something had to be done to stop them.

Bad blood between law enforcement and Ringo continued to escalate after he was accused of delivering a crippling gunshot wound to Virgil Earp on December 28, 1881—a couple of months after the shoot-out at the O.K. Corral. Then, on March 18, 1882, Morgan Earp was assassinated which gave rise to the historic, three-week "Vendetta Ride" in search of the perpetrator. Ringo denied having anything to do with Morgan's death, but just in case the Earps and their friend "Doc" Holliday believed otherwise, he hightailed it towards the hamlet of Galeyville. On July 14, 1882, Johnny Ringo was found dead in Morse's Canyon in the Chiricahua Mountains in Arizona Territory. He was discovered by teamster John Yoast leaning up against an oak tree with a bullet hole in his head; his boots were off and he held a .45 Colt revolver in his hand. It was reported that he had committed suicide, but the wife of Wyatt Earp, after his death in 1929, confessed that Wyatt and Doc Holliday had killed the legendary outlaw. John Peters Ringo was laid to rest on the spot and his grave was covered over with rocks.

Whether the legendary lawmen actually killed Johnny Ringo is still debated, but what is certain is that Ringo lived a wild life in the Old West and rubbed shoulders with many famous characters on both sides of the law.

As the Western era started to fad away in the rear view mirror, big shows starring iconic individuals began touring the country and overseas to roaring crowds. There were shows like Buffalo Bill's Wild West Show, the Miller Brothers' 101 Ranch Real Wild West, and Pawnee Bill's Pioneer Days. Paying customers saw great nostalgic shows and talented marksmen, like Phoebe Ann Moses (better known as "Annie Oakley"), who won her first shooting contest when she was only fifteen years old. She went on to wed Frank Butler, another sharpshooter who ended up taking a backseat to Oakley and began to manage her. The two eventually joined up with Buffalo Bill Cody's show in 1885 and toured until 1901. Oakley was honored to perform for Queen Victoria while the show was in Europe in 1887. From the early 1880s to the 1930s, there were over one hundred Western shows that sprang into existence trying to wow and dazzle the crowds—pining and yearning over the loss of the Old, Wild West. RTJ

Shades of the Old, Wild West

Scalper James Kirker: Genocide and Western Expansion

AFTER MEXICO won their independence from Spain in 1821, the flag of Mexico proudly flew over much of America's West Coast and Southwest. By the 1830s, the temptation of a lucrative bounty upon the heads of Mexicans and Native Americans in the Southwest lured many whites to the region to try their luck at human scalping to make money; however, many others flocked to the area for avarice land-grabbing. Unfortunately, during the expansion period and western migration of the whites many Mexicans and Indians were tortured, raped, relocated, and murdered.

The idea of scalp-hunting was nothing new to America, in Salem, Massachusetts, for instance, the walls inside the courthouse were once adorned with Indian scalps which had been turned-in for bounties; the courthouse was eventually razed in 1785 and the macabre, public display was finally retired. The heinous work of scalping in the Southwest was once referred to as "barbering," while the western expansionism of the United States was inspired by the clever catchphrase "Manifest Destiny"—the notion that God had awarded the nation from sea to shining sea to white supremacy. However, the indigenous inhabitants in protecting their homes and firesides were also known to comment acts of barbarism.

From the scalping-for-profit era of the nineteenth century, there arose an American icon that came to be known as the "King of the

SHADES OF THE OLD, WILD WEST

Scalpers," his name was James Kirker. Kirker was born in 1793 in the small Irish hamlet of Kilcross to Rose and Gilbert Kirker. Growing up in County Antrim just north of Belfast, young James would have probably enjoyed the county's Giant Causeway (more than 40,000 hexagonal formations created by molten lava), castle ruins, beautiful scenic coastlines, and the farms that dotted the "Emerald Isle's" landscape of Northern Ireland.

Kirker eventually left Ireland and sailed to America in 1810. During the War of 1812, he served as a privateer aboard the *Black Joke*, disrupting British shipping for the United States. After the war was over, Kirker met and married Catharine Dunigan who was also of Irish decent; however, in 1817 Kirker, for some reason, left his wife behind and headed west to St. Louis. Located at the Missouri River and Mississippi River confluence, St. Louis was a bustling town flourishing in the fur trading industry—championing the Western trade. The town's wharf was continually lined with steamboats which catered to the multitudes and their goods and supplies headed to and from the beaver country in the West—and, later, the stampede of those heading to the Western mines and goldfields populated the town even more, which made St. Louis the "Gateway to the West."

The call of further "Westering" overtime got the better of Kirker and he joined a 100-wagon train bound west over the Santa Fe Trail. After arriving in New Mexico, he eventually got involved in helping to protect convoys of copper ore crossing Apache territory. The Apache were hell-bent on protecting and maintaining their lands against all intruders. They resisted those trespassing on the Santa Fe Trail and the Butterfield Overland Mail and Stagecoach Route. These fierce-fighting warriors of the Southwest had adopted the equestrian lifestyle of the Spanish who had invaded and colonized the region. Two of the tribes most celebrated leaders was Geronimo and Cochise—resisting to the end, the Apache were the last American Indians to surrender to the United States government. However, in order to protect his convoys, Kirker made friends with some of the tribal Indian chiefs which angered the Mexicans. As a result, the governor of New Mexico Territory issued an arrest warrant on Kirker which prompted him to flee to Bent's Fort in

Colorado.

Bent's Fort was located on the north bank of the Arkansas River near the junction of the Purgatoire River a few miles east of present-day La Junta, Colorado. The outpost enjoyed a bustling business at this cross-trailed junction. Since 1833 when the Bent brothers, William and Charles, along with their partner, Ceran St. Vrain, Native Americans and various rough and rugged mountain men traded and found refuge within the fort's walls. While Kirker was at Bent's Fort, he met and befriended Spybuck, a Shawnee Indian. When word arrived that the governor of New Mexico Territory had been beheaded, Kirker decided to return there with his comrade, Spybuck. Back in New Mexico Territory, Kirker gathered together an army in 1839 of about fifty Indian warriors—Delaware and Shawnee, to "lift" Mexican and Apache scalps at $100 each for males, $50 for women, and $25 for children. To keep Kirker and others on the job, the bounty was later raised to $200 for a warrior's scalp. The genocide, to rid the coveted territory of its indigenous inhabitants, still haunts American history.

The coming of the Mexican War in 1846 enticed the King of the Scalpers to join the ranks where he served as a scout and guide under Colonel Alexander W. Doniphan. Col. Doniphan hailed from Liberty, Missouri, and was in command of the First Missouri Volunteers under Colonel Stephen Watts Kearny.

Col. Kearny was born on August 30, 1794, in Newark, New Jersey, and after joining the military he rose in rank and was sent to Fort Bellefontaine near St. Louis; a couple of months later he was sent to construct the Jefferson Barracks which was just downriver from Fort Bellefontaine; two years after that, he found himself in command of Fort Crawford in Wisconsin. He married Mary Radford, stepdaughter of William Clark, of the famous Lewis and Clark fame, and before long Col. Kearny became commander of the Army of the West and was dubbed "Father of the U.S. Cavalry." Later, Kearny was eventually promoted to brigadier general.

In 1846 Col. Kearny was training his Missouri troops along the banks of the Missouri River getting prepared for a war with Mexico. Leaving Fort Leavenworth, Kansas, with a force of about 1,700

SHADES OF THE OLD, WILD WEST

men, they plodded along for about two months down the Santa Fe Trail and into history. By August 18, 1846, the Army of the West marched into Santa Fe where Col. Kearny addressed its conquered inhabitants and said: "I have come among you by the orders of my government, to take possession of your country and extend over it the laws of the United States. We come among you for your benefit, not for your injury." The city of Santa Fe fell without a single shot fired. Col. Kearny quickly became its military governor and set about establishing a legal code and a civil government for the new American territory. In the first month of 1847, after fighting in a few more engagements on the coast, California had followed in New Mexico's footsteps. The work had added another priceless piece to the map-makers Manifest Destiny puzzle.

Apache Chief Geronimo managed to outlive Kirker's scalping-knife, and through much of the 1880s he continued to terrorize white settlers and soldiers. Geronimo and thirty-six other followers, faced with about five thousand United States troops, finally surrendered at Skeleton Canyon in extreme southeastern Arizona in 1886. Chief Geronimo and about five hundred other Apaches were then taken to a U.S. military prison in Florida—they had lost their lands and freedom.

As for Kirker, he eventually wound up in Contra Costa County, California, just east of San Francisco. He lived there for almost three years and died in 1852 of natural causes.

The Treaty of Guadalupe Hildalgo, signed just north of Mexico City, ended the Mexico War and gave the United States "in addition to the disputed strip between the Nueces and the Rio Grande, California and the territory of the east including what is now Nevada, Utah, most of Arizona and New Mexico, and parts of Wyoming and Colorado. This region contained 529,000 square miles of new territory and ranked next in size to the Louisiana Purchase. The treaty with Mexico extended the southern boundary of Texas to the Rio Grande…The southern boundary of Arizona and New Mexico was completed by the Gadsden purchase (1853) of 30,000 square miles of territory…."

About the genocide and the reports and opinions during the nineteenth century, author and historian David Saville Muzzey

Scalper James Kirker

The Alamo

(Illustration from: *History of Our Country*, Reuben Post Halleck, American Book Company, New York, 1923.)

(In San Antonio, Texas, about 5,000 regular Mexican troops under General Santa Anna laid siege to the Alamo, an old Franciscan mission, starting on February 26, 1836. For 12 days the Mexican forces bombarded the strong walls of the old Spanish mission fort with intense artillery fire. At dawn on March 6, 1836, the Mexicans gave the bugle call *degnello*, which meant "fire and death," and stormed the Alamo. Inside were 187 defenders dead: Colonel William B. Travis lay where he fell with his rifle still in hand; Colonel James Bowie was bayoneted to death still lying on his cot; while Colonel Davy Crockett was discovered mutilated. Gen. Santa Anna gave orders to pile and burn the remains of all the Texas defenders.)

reported that: "One of the most serious problems of the period was the control of the Indians on our frontier from Montana to Texas. Resenting the invasion of their immemorial hunting-grounds by the steady westward migration of the 'pale faces,' they ambushed the stagecoaches, tore up rails, threw down telegraph poles, and massacred the inmates of the government posts…The Indian Bureau and the War Department were at loggerheads, each accusing the other of inefficiency and inhumanity. Commission Taylor of the bureau asserted in 1867 that it had cost the government over $40,000,000 to conduct the campaign of 1865; and that at the present rate of extermination [genocide] it would take twenty-five thousand years, at a cost of $300,000,000,000, to be rid of the 'red fiends.'"

On May 10, 1876, thousands of Americans attended the Philadelphia (Pennsylvania) Exposition celebrating the 100-year celebration of the United States. The "City of Brotherly Love" had created a 284-acre park to host exhibits of American advances in art, inventions, manufacturing and much, much more. Bells chimed and cannons roared as President Ulysses S. Grant declared the opening of the nation's Centennial Exhibition to the masses. In contrast, the very next month on June 25, 1876, General George Armstrong Custer and his force of 264 men were massacred by Sioux warriors under Chief Sitting Bull at the Little Bighorn.

Bibliography

Amsler, Kevin, *Final Resting Place: The Lives and Deaths of Famous St. Louisans*, Virginia Publishing Company, St. Louis, Missouri, 1997.

Arthur, Anthony, *General Jo Shelby's March*, Random House, New York, N.Y., 2010.

Dungan, Myles, *How the Irish Won the West*, Skyhorse Publishing, 2011.

Halleck, Reuben Post, *History of Our Country*, American Book Company, New York, 1923.

Hopkin, Alannah, *Berlitz Handbook Ireland*, Berlitz Publishing, London, 2012.

Muzzey, David Saville, *The United States of America II: From the Civil War*, Ginn and Company, Boston, 1924.

Parrish, William E.; Jones, Charles T.; and Christensen, Lawrence O., *Missouri: The Heart of the Nation*, Forum Press, Inc., Arlington Heights, Illinois, 1980.

Roark, James L., *The American Promise: A History of the United States*, Bedford Books, Boston, 1998.

Sides, Hampton, *Blood and Thunder: The Epic Story of Kit Carson and the Conquest of the American West*, Anchor Books, New York, N.Y., 2006.

Wallis, Michael, *The Wild West 365*, Abrams, New York, N.Y., 2011.

Wexler, Bruce, *How the Wild West was Won, A Celebration of Cowboys, Gunfighters, Buffalo Soldiers, Sodbusters, Moonshiners, and the American Frontier*, Skyhorse Publishing, New York, N.Y., 2013.

Winn, Christopher, *I Never Knew That About the Irish*, Thomas Dunne Books, St. Martin's Press, New York, N.Y., 2012.

Joaquin Murietta: Robin Hood of El Dorado

AFTER James Wilson Marshal's discovery of gold at Johann (John) Augustus Sutter's sawmill on the American River near Coloma, California, the rush for untold riches and avarice was underway. Hordes of gold-seeking individuals from near and far poured-in to the Golden State to try their luck at fortune. The stampede was fully realized after a man by the name of Samuel (Sam) Brannan, founder of the California *Star* newspaper, had the brilliant idea to advertise the gold strike by running through the streets of San Francisco crying out: "Gold! Gold on the American River!" Brannan's unusual marketing stunt did what the newspapers failed to do, and the California Gold Rush was born. Before the end of 1849, California was home and fireside to one hundred thousand "Forty-niners." As a result, towns and camps sprang up overnight to cater to the ever-increasing flood of riff-raff. Along with all the other want-to-be rich people was a man who would later be known as the "Robin Hood of El Dorado."

Joaquin Murietta was born in Sonora, Mexico, in 1832 and attended school in Mexico City. He married Carmen Rosita (another source maintains that her name was Antonia Molinera), and after catching the gold fever "bug", Murietta and his bride headed for the mining boom in California. By 1850 Murietta had established a claim in Stanislaus County near San Jose, but the treatment of Mexicans, Native Americans, and others in California's pro-Anglo climate left Murietta angry and very bitter. As the story goes—once,

SHADES OF THE OLD, WILD WEST

Illustration of Joaquin Murietta.

Joaquin Murietta

upon returning home to his cabin, he found that Carmen had been assaulted, raped, and murdered, his half-brother lynched, and his mining claim jumped. For Murietta, this was the last straw; he turned to a life of revenge and crime and never looked back over his shoulder.

Rage-filled Murietta teamed-up with a hombre named Manuel Garcia, better known as "Three-Fingered Jack," along with Reyes Feliz and, oddly enough, four other Joaquins—last names Valenzuela, Botellier, Ocomorenia, and Carrillo. Sometimes this brigand of Mexicans was referred to as the "Five Joaquins." From 1850 to 1853 Murietta's gang terrorized the Sierra Nevada region with home invasions, rustling livestock, holding up stagecoaches, murdering miners, and robbing isolated saloons. Reportedly, the Mexican Robin Hood once boarded a riverboat steamer on the Sacramento River and killed a number of the boat's crewmen, making off with about $20,000 in gold; another time, Murietta was said to have taken a herd of prize Spanish horses belonging to the governor; and many poor people who were down and out claimed that the bandit was generous and shared his bounty with them—fueling the Zorro-like legend.

Finally, on May 11, 1853, the state legislature decided they had had enough of this mountain robber and, as a result, California's governor, John Bigler, placed a bounty of $5,000 on Murietta's head—dead or alive. The California State Rangers under Captain Harry Love, who had served as a Texas Ranger, army scout, noted gunfighter, and deputy sheriff of Los Angeles was sent to apprehend the gang.

However, down in Texas, law enforcement was organized in the 1820s when Texas was still part of Spanish Territory. Following in Moses Austin's footsteps, his son, Stephen Fuller Austin, continued what his father had started in the territory and went on to secure land for white settlement. The first American colony in the region grew to about 14,000 whites and about 400 slaves by 1825. The need for some type of law and order prompted Austin to form a small group of volunteers, which he dubbed "Rangers." Ironic, though, these Americans did not see slavery as unlawful. They were forced, however, to be Mexicans and Catholic. In time, this

SHADES OF THE OLD, WILD WEST

temporary Ranger solution eventually became known as the "Texas Rangers" after Texas won its independence from Mexico.

California's need to also quell its lawlessness came to a head, many thanks to the Murietta gang, and led to the formation of the California State Rangers. Led by Captain Harry Love, the new organization of law enforcers was given the difficult and dangerous task of apprehending or killing the wanted desperadoes. Capt. Love and his Rangers, investigating a column of smoke rising above the San Joaquin Valley on July 25, 1853, had discovered Murietta's campfire. Basking in the glow of the firelight the outlaws were surprised by the lawmen and a deadly shootout erupted. After the fireside smoke had given way to the gunfire smoke, the mission of Capt. Love and his lawmen was over—the proof and evidence of their death-dealing justice would take the form of Murietta's severed head and the severed three-fingered hand of Three-Fingered Jack.

The macabre collection was then gathered-up by one of the Rangers, Billy Henderson, and temporarily preserved in whiskey and taken back to civilization. The trophies were then auctioned off with the head fetching $35. They were eventually stored in glass jars of alcohol and displayed throughout the state as a gruesome, money-making sideshow—in jailhouses, saloons, mining camps, and other places. The jar containing the head of Murietta eventually wound-up in a museum in San Francisco on Market Street for about forty years until it became a casualty of the Great Earthquake of 1906.

On April 18, 1906, at 5:13 a.m. in the wee hours of the morning, San Francisco experienced a history-making disaster. Violent quakes cracked open and split highways, caused steel buildings to shake and sway, and also destroyed and devastated many homes and businesses. There were six massive shockwaves with the third one being the worst of all. Many people perished under the rubble, while fire consumed eight square miles of the area including hundreds of city blocks. Almost 250,000 citizens were made homeless, and the destruction caused hundreds of thousands of dollars in damage. The head of Murietta was lost, as a result, and so ended the freak show.

Over the years stories and films were produced. In 1854 a writer

Joaquin Murietta

from San Francisco, John Rollin Ridge, wrote a fictional tale about Murietta as a Robin Hood-type character that robbed the rich in order to help the poor. The racism that permeated California at the time helped to fuel the popularity of such a book, and many other novels followed.

In 1919 a "hack-writer" for pulp periodicals, Johnson McCulley, at a penny a word, created the popular character Zorro (Spanish for "fox"). The Mexican hero, who always humiliated his adversaries with his incredible swordsmanship, wowed, dazzled, and entertained the public. McCulley first introduced Zorro in "The Curse of Capistrano" which was later renamed the "Mark of Zorro"—it eventually became a huge, smash hit at the box office.

The Robin Hood of El Dorado, who sought to exact revenge for the wrongs perpetrated upon him, his family, and his people, by violence and other lawless methods, left a history that continues to stir the mind. The argument is still alive and well today in many and various ways, and the solutions are oftentimes blurred, hidden, or exposed, but the tales and stories are ongoing—with many yet untold.

SHADES OF THE OLD, WILD WEST

Chronology

1832—Joaquin Murietta (or Murieta) was born in Sonora, Mexico.

1849—before the end of the year California would have about one hundred thousand "Forty-niners" as a result of the Gold Rush.

1850—Murietta had established a mining claim in Stanislaus County near San Jose, California.

1850-1853—Murietta and his gang was terrorizing the Sierra Nevada region and the state legislature decides to intervene.

July 25, 1853—Captain Harry Love and his California Rangers discovered the campsite of Murietta and his outlaws, including Three-Fingered Jack, and a firefight ensues—for proof of their deaths, Murietta's head is removed as well as the three-fingered hand of Three-Fingered Jack.

April 18, 1906—The Great Earthquake of California occurs in the San Francisco area which destroys the jar of alcohol that contained the head of Murietta—it had been used as a sideshow for over 50 years.

Joaquin Murietta

Bibliography

Athearn, Robert G., *American Heritage: New Illustrated History of the United States*, Vol. 6, *The Frontier*, Fawcett Publications, Inc., One Astor Plaza, New York, N.Y., 1963.

Enss, Chris, *Outlaw Tales of California: True Stories of the Golden State's Most Infamous Crooks, Culprits, and Cutthroats*, Twodot, Guilford, Connecticut, 2013.

Jackson, Rex T., *Timeless Stories of the West: Mountaineers, Miners, and Indians*, Heritage Books, Inc., Berwyn Heights, Maryland, 2016.

Legrand, Jacques, *Chronicle of America*, Chronicle Publications, Inc., Mount Kisco, New York, 1989.

Mayo, Matthew P., *Sourdoughs, Claim Jumpers & Dry Gulchers: Fifty of the Grittiest Moments in the History of Frontier Prospecting*, Twodot, Globe Pequot Press, Guilford, Connecticut, 2012.

McNab, Chris, *Gunfighters: The Outlaws and Their Weapons*, Thunder Bay Press, San Diego, California, 2005.

Turner, George, *Gun Fighters*, L. Baxter Lane Publisher, Amarillo, Texas, 1972.

Wallis, Michael, *The Wild West 365*, Abrams, New York, N.Y., 2011

Other sources:

Columbia Tristar Home Entertainment, *The Mask of Zorro*, (DVD documentary), 1998.

William Tilghman: Legendary Lawman

THE WEST was a hellhole of lawlessness during the nineteenth century—especially in Indian Territory (Oklahoma). Western expansionism, which rode on the coattails of "Manifest Destiny," as well as the promise of homesteading, employment, and the allure of gold and silver, brought the multitudes westward. Along with the massive horde of humanity came riff-raff as well, and many deplorable, criminal-minded people took full advantage of a vulnerable country without regulations and adequate law and order. It was a dangerous place for a number of reasons, but it promised all the things which truly constituted the Wild West.

As a result of the speed in which the West became populated, the lack of good law enforcement was just as quickly realized by the more innocent citizen. And so the type and sort of individuals that answered the call of the dangerous service had to be as tough and rugged as the situation demanded. In this environment, the lines between an Old West lawman and an outlaw were oftentimes blurred, and a number of them were known to court both sides of the law. The temptations that flourished in those old Western towns could corrupt even the most lawful citizen into questionable territory. However, out of the many historical figures who had the courage and nerve to wear a badge in the West, one name repeatedly rises to the top of the list, his name was William Tilghman.

William (Bill) Matthew Tilghman Jr. was born on July 4, 1854, in Fort Dodge, Iowa, which is located at the confluence of the

SHADES OF THE OLD, WILD WEST

Illustration of William Matthew Tilghman.

William Tilghman

Lizard and Des Moines rivers. He was raised on a farm where poverty ruled the roost. Growing up, young Bill would have probably been no stranger to the hard work and chores associated with that sort of lifestyle—caring for livestock, planting and harvesting, hunting and all the other things common to such simplistic living. However, like with most children, they eventually grow up and turn their attention to their own futures, and Bill Tilghman was no exception to the rule. By 1871 he had ventured west to Kansas and began hunting buffalo for a living.

Tilghman would "hang his hat" in Dodge City, a town known as the "Western Babylon" and also the "Cowboy Capital." From the early part of the 1870s, he hunted buffalo, operated the Crystal Palace Saloon, and served as a deputy. Dodge City was laid out in 1872 by A.A. Robinson and named after Colonel Richard I. Dodge who was in command of nearby Fort Dodge; the fort was located about five miles from the town. Much of the hubbub that surrounded Dodge City was due to the fact that the town was situated close to the Santa Fe Trail, the end of the railhead, and the place where thousands of longhorn cattle were driven overland from Texas. Along with this activity, however, came high-strung drovers that were hell-bent on having a good time after being on the long, hard, dusty trail. It also attracted many other individuals, like preachers and con artists, gamblers, drunkards, thieves, prostitutes, and many others; there were entrepreneurs, craftsmen, job seekers, settlers, tourists, soldiers, hunters, and the list goes on.

During the time Tilghman served as a lawman in Dodge City under Bartholomew (Bat) Masterson, using tactics like outlawing firearms north of the railroad tracks, the town was, for the most part, cleared of unsavory troublemakers. The local cemetery, Boot Hill, received its name on account of the many lawless souls that died with their boots on, which may have also been somewhat of a deterrent to lawbreakers. Other such well-known lawmen of Dodge City include: Jack Bridges, Billy Brooks, Ed and Bat Masterson, Wyatt Earp, Ben Daniels, "Mysterious" Dave Mather, Luke Short, Charley Bassett and others.

The stories and tales surrounding such Wild West icons were many, for instance, after Bat Masterson was elected sheriff of

SHADES OF THE OLD, WILD WEST

Dodge City in 1877 he had to endure the death of his brother Ed at the hands of Jack Wagner and Alf Walker. Ed's funeral was the biggest one the town had ever seen, and after his beloved sibling had been laid to rest, Bat tracked down the two, responsible desperadoes and killed them dead.

Another example in Dodge City involved Dave Mather, who was a wild and wooly character that had a bad reputation that some were tempted to judge as an ungodly sinner. As the story goes, a Christian preacher decided to visit Dodge City on a self-appointed mission to convert the vilest soul in what he considered to be "sin city." Many of the Christians in town felt that if such a man as Mysterious Dave Mather could be saved from the jaws of hell, they could die happy with the knowledge; and the minister also said that if Mather could be converted he too would be ready to face the Almighty and not shrink back.

It just so happened church was being held that very night at the Lady Gay Dance Hall, and Mather was seated in the front row. After the preacher had delivered his spirited sermon, Mather rose and admitted that he had had a miraculous rebirth and said that "since we've all judged ourselves to be saved we might as well go straight to heaven and leave this sinful, hellhole behind." Mather drew his pistol and proceeded to shoot out all the dance hall lanterns. As a result, the preacher wasted no time diving out of the nearest window while the other churchgoers quickly crawled for cover. Mather, seeing that they preferred flesh to spirit and hellhole to heaven, left the dance hall a wiser man. After that incident, no one dared condemn or preach to Dave Mather.

In 1889, Tilghman relocated to Oklahoma and during the 1890s he tracked down many criminals wanted by the law. One of these hardened public enemies was Bill Doolin, who was once part of the infamous Dalton Gang. The Dalton's were made famous by the daring two-bank robbery attempt at Coffeyville, Kansas, on October 5, 1892. Bob, Grat, and Emmett Dalton, along with Bill Powers and Dick Broadwell, rode boldly into Coffeyville that fateful morning where Grat, Broadwell and Powers entered the Condon Bank and Bob and Emmett the First National Bank. During the time the heists were underway the townspeople, noticing the strangers, made ready to give them a warm reception when they exited the banks. A blazing showdown occurred when the gang was making their getaway with the loot. In the end, several of the town's brave defenders died and only one of the outlaws survived the ordeal— Emmett. For some reason, Bill Dalton and Bill Doolin did not participate in the Coffeyville robbery. From this point, however, Doolin would take the lead and form the Doolin Gang, sometimes referred to as the "Oklahombres."

Tilghman would have his hands full bringing these outlaws to justice, the gang mostly consisted of Bill Dalton, "Red Buck" Weightman, Dan "Dynamite Dick" Clifton, "Little" Dick West, Roy "Arkansas Tom" Daugherty, "Little" Bill Raidler, William "Tulsa Jack" Blake, George "Bitter Creek" Newcomb, Alf Sohn, Bob Grounds, Charley Pierce and Ole Yantis. In order to get control over the rampant lawlessness in Oklahoma Indian Territory, Tilghman had a lot of help; most of it came from Judge Isaac C. Parker, also known as the "Hanging Judge" who was appointed by President Ulysses S. Grant to Fort Smith, Arkansas; he would go on to serve a twenty-one year jurisdiction there. Judge Parker would employ many United States marshals—the most famous was what became known as the "Three Guardsmen." The trio was made up of Tilghman; and Heck Thomas, a Southern veteran of the American Civil War who fought under Confederate General Robert E. Lee when he was at the tender age of only twelve; and last but not least was Chris Madsen, who reportedly served in the French Foreign Legion and in the American West as a soldier and Indian fighter.

The law responded to numerous crimes perpetrated throughout the region, but the Doolin Gang faced a close call on September 1, 1893, at Ingalls, Oklahoma, in an Old Western-style gun-battle that has been compared to the shootout at the O.K. Corral. The Doolin Gang somehow escaped with the exception of Arkansas Tom who was captured.

An example of the Doolin Gang's outlawry might best be represented by the bank robbery at Southwest City, Missouri, on May 10, 1894. Doolin and his Oklahombres rode into unsuspecting Southwest City and dismounted behind the post office and tied up their horses. According to the Southwest City *Enterprise* quoted in

SHADES OF THE OLD, WILD WEST

BANK ROBBERY.

The Bank of Southwest City Robbed of $3,700.

[Southwest City Enterprise, Friday, May 11.]

At about 3:30 o'clock yesterday afternoon seven well armed men rode into town from the south and dismounted in the street, just back of the postoffice, and tied their horses. Three of them made their way immediately to the bank, while the other four took positions, two in the pool hall, just north and across the street from the postoffice, while the other two stood in Dr. Nichols' yard. The first words heard from them was an order for everybody to hunt holes, accompanied by an oath. To give their language more force they began firing their winchesters, and kept up a fusilade. The men proceeded to the bank, and covered Mr. Ault, the owner of the bank, and Mr. Snyder, an assistant, with revolvers. Two of the men immediately crawled through the cashier's window, while the third held revolvers on Mr Snyder and Mr. Ault. After relieving the vault and cashier's drawer of the money, they deposited it in a sack and made their way to their horses, keeping up a

Headlines from the Neosho *Times*, May 17, 1894.

the Neosho *Times* dated May 17, 1894, "Three of them made their way immediately to the bank while the other four took positions, two in the pool hall...and...two stood in Doctor Nichols' yard...."

The *Enterprise* reported that the robbers gave the "order for everybody to hunt holes, accompanied by an oath. To give their language more force, they began firing their Winchesters, and kept up a fusillade."

While their weapons were being trained on A.F. Ault, the bank owner, and his assistant, Mr. Snyder, a couple of the outlaws "crawled through the cashier's window."

The crooks snatched up all the money they could find in the bank vault and cashier's drawer, and stuffed it in a bag and dashed for their mounts and their getaway "keeping up a constant firing at everyone who dared to show his head."

Meanwhile, outside in the street, the four "were doing deadly execution with their Winchesters." They were buying precious escape-time for their cohorts in the bank with their red hot lead.

The brazen bandits made off with about $3,700, but not before they wounded J.C. Seabourne, an ex-State Senator, who was with his brother, Oscar, along with M.V. Hembree, and Deputy U.S. Marshal Simpson Melton. It was reported that a total of "100 shots were fired on Main Street and sounded like war times [Civil War], and many citizens had very close calls from the robbers' guns."

As the Doolin Gang headed south on Broadway Street they received a "warm reception" from City Marshal Carlyle, D.E. Havens, G.W. Smith, E.W. Eslinger and S. Melton; Charles Franks and Dick Prater also dished out a "dose as they passed the Baptist Church."

As a result of the gunplay, J.C. Seabourne did not recover but died a few days later from his wounds. Oscar survived but Hembree lost his foot above the ankle.

The Oklahombres paused about fourteen miles south of Southwest City, took care of their injuries and had something to eat. It was later ascertained that six of the seven bandits were wounded in some way during the historic shootout and getaway. They eventually rode through nearby Creek and Cherokee territories to put more distance between them and their crime.

SHADES OF THE OLD, WILD WEST

After Doolin contracted rheumatism he decided to make haste to Eureka Springs, Arkansas, for some of the popular mineral baths that the mountainous retreat was famous for. Unknown to Doolin, however, Tilghman was hot on his trail.

The town of Eureka Springs, located in northwest Arkansas, was founded by Judge L.B. Saunders. He traveled there and discovered the Eureka Springs' "Basin Spring," where he built a small house there in 1879. Before long, many others came from near and far and upon testing the "water that healed" exclaimed: "Eureka!"—which means "I have found it!" Eureka Springs would come to be known as the "City of Healing Waters." The very reason that the outlaw sought out all that it had to offer.

Marshal Tilghman, after having intercepted a letter, connected the dots and headed for Arkansas. He arrived there on January 15, 1896, and wisely tried to keep a low profile while asking around for Doolin's whereabouts. After learning that he was in a particular bathhouse, Tilghman entered and confronted Doolin. A struggle ensued and the lawman won, arresting the outlaw.

Doolin was taken back to Guthrie, Oklahoma, and incarcerated awaiting trial. Not to be kept from his exciting life of lawlessness and crime, he masterminded a daring jailbreak on July 5, 1896, with several other yahoos and then went into hiding for awhile. On August 25, 1896, Bill Doolin was gunned down by "Guardsman" Heck Thomas in a deadly duel near Lawson, Oklahoma—Doolin shot twice and Thomas only fired his shotgun once. His riddled body was displayed on a mortuary slab and then buried in the Boot Hill section of Guthrie's Summit View Cemetery.

All things earthly must come to an end and for Bill Tilghman the same was true. Finally, after serving for over fifty years, the old lawman of the West died in the line of duty with his boots on at the ripe age of seventy. It was October 31, 1924, outside Ma Murphy's Dance Hall in Cromwell, Oklahoma, and Tilghman was attempting to arrest an intoxicated man, Wiley Lynn, who was disturbing the peace. Lynn produced an unexpected pistol from his pocket and poured two bullets in Tilghman's chest—he didn't live long. His body was taken to Oklahoma City where it lay in state in the capital rotunda for three days. Thousands of onlookers turned out for one last look at the historic icon that had served for so long bringing in dangerous criminals to face justice or rehabilitation; the mourners also included a United States senator, governor, ex-governors, and many others.

In his life Bill Tilghman also had a softer side, he had married twice. His first wife was Flora Kendall who died in 1900 of tuberculosis; they were married in 1877. His second wife, Zoe Stratton, which he married on July15, 1903, outlived her husband and became a successful author who went on to write a book about her beloved husband titled *Marshal of the Last Frontier: The Life and Service of William Matthew Tilghman*.

Another interesting fact about Tilghman is that in 1915 he served as a director and actor and teamed-up with E.D. Nix and Chris Madsen and made a film called *The Passing of the Oklahoma Outlaws*; his first attempt, however, was a nineteen minute film which was titled *The Bank Robbery*.

The man that was dubbed one of the greatest peace officers of the American West, who brought to justice and sent many outlaws to the hoosegow, and was known to have been a gentle and soft-spoken individual, left a legacy that continues to inspire the living with his heroic tales of the Old, Wild West.

Chronology

July 4, 1854—William Matthew Tilghman was born in Fort Dodge, Iowa.

1870s—Tilghman relocates to Kansas and begins making a living hunting buffalos and also serves as a lawman in Dodge City under Bat Masterson.

1889—Tilghman relocates to Oklahoma.

1890s—Tilghman tracks down many outlaws during this time as part of the "Three Guardsman" sent out by Judge Isaac Parker of Fort Smith, Arkansas.

January 15, 1896—Tilghman arrests Bill Doolin at a bathhouse in Eureka Springs, Arkansas.

October 31, 1924—Bill Tilghman is gunned down in front of a dance hall in Cromwell, Oklahoma.

Bibliography

Anderson, Dan, and Yadon, Laurence, *100 Oklahoma Outlaws, Gangsters, and Lawmen 1839-1939*, Pelican Publishing Company, Gretna, Louisiana, 2007.

Enss, Chris, *More Tales Behind the Tombstones: More Deaths and Burials of the Old West's Most Nefarious Outlaws, Notorious Women, and Celebrated Lawmen*, Twodot, Guilford, Connecticut, 2014.

Jackson, Rex T., *Traces of Ozarks Past: Outlaws, Icons, and Memorable Events*, Heritage Books, Inc., Berwyn Heights, Maryland, 2013; *Monumental Tales from the Ozarks*, Heritage Books, Inc., Berwyn Heights, Maryland, 2015.

Marriott, Barbara, *Outlaw Tales of New Mexico: True Stories of the Land of Enchantment's Most Infamous Crooks, Culprits, and Cutthroats*, Twodot, Guilford, Connecticut, 2007.

Raine, William MacLeod, *Famous Sheriffs and Western Outlaws: Incredible True Stories of Wild West Showdowns and Frontier Justice*, Skyhorse Publishing, Inc., New York, N.Y., 2012.

Turner, George, *Gun Fighters*, Baxter Lane Company, Amarillo, Texas, 1972.

Wallis, Michael, *The Wild West 365*, Abrams, New York, N.Y., 2011.

Wexler, Bruce, *How the West was Won: A Celebration of Cowboys, Gunfighters, Buffalo Soldiers, Sodbusters, Moonshiners, and the American Frontier*, Skyhorse Publishing, New York, N.Y., 2013.

Other Sources:

Southwest City *Enterprise*, May 11, 1894.
Neosho *Times*, May 17, 1894.

Pinkertons, Gads Hill, and the Showdown-Shootout at Roscoe

AMERICA'S Civil War produced a number of heroes and villains on both sides. After the war, some were able to go home to a patriot's welcome while others were not. The options available for those who faced ridicule and retaliation was limited. As a result, some of the best of the worst, if you choose to view in this way, dove into a life of crime—robbing banks, express offices, trains, and citizens.

Just a little north of Roscoe, Missouri, in St. Clair County is a roadside monument that commemorates a deadly nineteenth century showdown-shootout. Besides offering information about this historic event, the stone marker directs its remote audience to a side-road where another smaller, older stone marker, almost obscure in a fence line, reveals the actual spot where the firefight occurred—and, even though the black powder smoke has long since dissipated and those days of Wild West outlawry and gunplay are nearly forgotten by most, this little-known historical site can still muster back to the mind that day when justice and lawlessness clashed in a blazing, death-dealing, lead-pouring conflict.

Prior to the American Civil War, the issue of slavery and equality had become a hotbed of trouble for the Border States of Kansas and Missouri. Kansas Jayhawkers, Redlegs, and abolitionists made raids into Missouri and terrorized their pro-

SHADES OF THE OLD, WILD WEST

Historic monument just north of Roscoe, Missouri.

Southern neighbors, who allowed this heinous, inhuman institution of slavery to continue; likewise, guerrillas and bushwhackers from Missouri, crossed over into Kansas for their own fiendish purposes. As a result, many citizens of Missouri joined the Confederacy of rebels when the War Between the States erupted in 1861, and its people aided and abetted invaders headed for Union Kansas. After the war in 1865, life was made difficult for ex-rebels as they were oppressed during "Reconstruction." And Yankee carpetbaggers were on hand to gobble up land when mortgages were not met, due to the hardships and persecutions of post-Civil War life.

Little wonder, that to this day, the outlaws that rose out of the ashes of that fiery era were, to some extent, glorified and revered by some as legends and heroes. Out of the need to apprehend them, however, Pinkerton Detectives were sent out to gamble their lives for the sake of bringing to justice the lawless misfits of that wild and rugged time.

In 1819, a man named Allan Pinkerton was born in Glasgow, Scotland. When he was young he immigrated to America, and by 1842 he had settled near Chicago, Illinois, and was elected county sheriff. In 1850 he established the Pinkerton National Detective Agency whose motto was: "We Never Sleep." While serving in law enforcement he gained the favor of President Abraham Lincoln after he uncovered an assassination plot against him. During the American Civil War, Pinkerton took charge of the Secret Service and further impressed President Lincoln gathering vital information in support of the Union. By the mid-1870s, however, the run-amuck lawlessness that followed the war prompted the outlaws' many victims to seek out the Pinkerton Detective Agency to help solve the crisis. Pinkerton's success as a detective earned him the name "The Eye," which would eventually lead to the term "private eye."

In Missouri, which many referred to as the "Outlaw State," the James-Younger Gang were causing quite a stir with their hit-and-run outlawry. In order to attempt to bring these ruthless, ex-Confederate guerrillas to justice, following a train robbery at Gads Hill, the Pinkerton Agency was contacted.

In the northwest corner of Wayne County is the tiny hamlet of Gads Hill, which was located on the Iron Mountain Railroad.

SHADES OF THE OLD, WILD WEST

Situated about thirty miles south of Pilot Knob and Fort Davidson, and Piedmont about seven miles to the south, Gads Hill enjoyed the tranquility of its beautiful Ozark Mountain surroundings. However, on January 31, 1874, at 5:40 in the afternoon, the little settlement— a railroad flag station, was facing five armed brigands hell-bent on robbing them and the train which was about to arrive.

First, they secured the depot and then set a signal flag to halt the oncoming passenger train. After the train had obeyed the signal and stopped at the platform, the bandits went to work with their weapons drawn to persuade the train conductor, fireman, and passengers that it was in their best interests to handover all of their valuables; they didn't stop there, the highwaymen also rifled through the mailbags and safe. When it was all said and done, the James-Younger Gang had gained several thousand dollars of treasure.

The train was sent on its merry way south in the direction of Little Rock, Arkansas, and the gang rode off pell-mell into the safety of the Ozark terrain. The train steamed-on as fast as it could go to nearby Piedmont and telegraphed the breaking news about their frightening experience. A posse was formed which tracked the James-Younger Gang as far as the Current River, but eventually lost the trail and gave up.

As a result of the Gads Hill affair the Pinkerton National Detective Agency was hired to solve the problem, one way or the other. Captain Louis J. Lull and James Wright (some sources say John Boyle) were dispatched from the agency to track them down.

Louis J. Lull was in the Union army during the Civil War and was serving as a captain on the Chicago police force when he was asked to hunt down the James-Younger Gang. James Wright, on the other hand, who was from St. Louis, Missouri, was thought to have served in the Confederate army with some men of St. Clair County, which might explain his actions during the coming battle at Roscoe.

After the posse gave up their search for the Gads Hill robbers, Lull and Wright picked up where they left off and wound up in the area of Monegaw Springs—not far from Roscoe. Monegaw Springs, in St. Clair County, was a popular resort and spa at the time, which also had caves along the Osage River where outlaws, such as the

Youngers, were known to haunt and hole up.

Monegaw Springs enjoyed a rich history because of its mineral springs. The first settlers to arrive in the area were the Appleton family in 1834. By 1852, a large three-and-one-half story log hotel was constructed there that overlooked the town's spring and passing river; however, the hotel burned down in 1926 which helped to bring much of the activity in Monegaw Springs to an end.

Not having any success, Lull and Wright searched some extreme western Missouri counties before returning to St. Clair County where they rented rooms at the Commercial Hotel in Osceola. While in the Osceola area, Captain Lull used an alias W.J. Allen. Posing as cattle buyers, as the story goes, they made the acquaintance of Edwin B. Daniels who was a deputy sheriff of St. Clair County. By sleuthing and poking around, the detectives were able to ascertain that Jim and John Younger were nearby staying at the home of Theodrick Snuffer, a friend of the Younger family. Deputy Daniels would accompany Lull and Wright since he knew the Osage River country well. The pursuers left Osceola on March 16, 1874, riding west toward Roscoe and into history.

Before long, they arrived in the small village of Roscoe about twelve miles west of Osceola and not far from Monegaw Springs. The trio spent the night in the Roscoe House, which was owned by Oliver Burch who had reportedly ridden beside guerrilla chieftain William Clarke Quantrill in the war. Pretending to be in the market for cattle, the men received information that the "Widow Sims" might have some of the beasts for sale, which would put them in the area they thought they needed to be. Leaving the Roscoe House at high noon they headed north on the Old Chalk Road.

After riding about two miles they headed east passing a little log school known as the Benton Green School, and on to the Snuffer home. Wright remained behind thinking that he might be recognized, while Lull and Deputy Daniels rode up to the gate. Old man Snuffer, whose sons were friends of the Youngers (Cole, Jim, Bob, and John), came out and told them the way to the Widow Sims'.

Meanwhile, inside the Snuffer house, Jim and John Younger were at the dinner table when the detectives arrived—it was around

SHADES OF THE OLD, WILD WEST

two o'clock, March 17, 1874. After hearing the hoof beats of the cattle buyers stopping to inquire the way to the Sims', the Youngers climbed a ladder into the upper portion of the house to peer out between the cracks in the logs when Snuffer went out to converse with the strange visitors.

When the Younger brothers observed that Lull and Daniels did not leave in the direction of the Sims' place, and that the strangers were loaded for bear, their suspicions were aroused. The brothers, armed with shotguns and pistols cut across country to the Chalk Level Road about a half mile from the house.

By this time, Wright had rejoined the other two and was near the two-story log cabin of John and Hannah McFerren, who were African Americans and also good friends of the Youngers. Suddenly, Lull, Wright, and Daniels heard the sounds of horse hooves pounding the rock-hard, Ozark ground and turned to see Jim and John Younger—some of the very men they were wanting to bring to justice.

The Youngers were prepared to do battle as John's double barrel shotgun was cocked and ready, while his brother Jim brandished a pistol. At this point, Wright spurred his horse and skedaddled but Jim, realizing that these men were no doubt lawmen and not really cattle buyers, shouted for him to stop. When Wright failed to heed his command, Jim fired his weapon shooting off the hat from the top of his head. Unharmed, Wright continued on east and out of view—riding hard!

The Youngers then ordered Lull and Deputy Daniels to disarm, and Jim dismounted his horse to retrieve their guns. As the Youngers were interrogating their adversaries, Lull, seizing an opportunity reached into his cape and pulled out a pistol and shot John Younger. The bullet hit John in the neck and damaged his jugular vein, though mortally wounded he managed to give Lull both barrels of his scattergun—hitting the Pinkerton's left shoulder and arm. Detective Lull then rode off toward the east with John somehow giving chase. Lull was taken out of his saddle by a low hanging branch and John was able at this point to catch up, squeezing off two rounds, one which pierced Captain Lull's chest. Still, John was able to ride back toward where his brother was.

Showdown-Shootout at Roscoe

While all of this was taking place, Jim was under fire by Osceola's Deputy Daniels, but as Daniels made an attempt to escape, Jim Younger shot him through the left side of his neck, and then headed in the direction of John. As John came into view, Jim could see his brother tottering in his saddle. Jim, probably fearing the worst thing that could happen to the Younger's youngest sibling, yelled to him, and John, as best he could gave him one last glance and fell from his horse over a fence into a pigpen across from the McFerren house. By the time Jim could reach him, John was dead.

Jim sent word to Snuffer to guard over John's body, by way of George McDonald who lived nearby and had arrived on the scene. Next, Jim took his brother's horse and rode west to the Chalk Road in hopes of picking up the trail of the Pinkerton Detective, James Wright, who had fled the scene at the outbreak of the heated showdown and gunplay.

Neighbor John Davis arrived as well to see what had transpired and discovered the lifeless body of Deputy Edwin Daniels; not far from him was the outlaw John Younger, who was also dead. A little further on Davis found Captain Louis Lull sitting up against a tree badly injured. Lull was carried to the McFerren cabin where his wounds were seared. Later that evening, he was taken to the Roscoe House at Roscoe for two local doctors to attend to his injuries—Dr. A.C. Marquis and Dr. L. Lewis.

Twenty-three days after the shootout it was reported that Lull had died and that his body was placed in a coffin, taken by wagon to Clinton, Missouri, and put on a train bound for Chicago where he was buried—but, some believed that he recovered.

As for the remains of John Younger, it was kept at the John McFerren house until the next morning when it was buried temporarily in a shallow grave near the Snuffer house under a cedar tree. That evening the body of the wanted outlaw was exhumed and taken a few miles southeast to the Old Yeater-Cleveland Cemetery and buried permanently in an unmarked grave with his head to the northwest and his feet to the southeast. Before long, Jim Younger went south to reunite with his other brothers, Cole and Bob, and to break the sad news of the loss of their little brother.

As a result of the killings of the Pinkerton agents and Deputy

Edwin Daniels, Missouri legislators appropriated ten thousand dollars to create an armed force of agents to help quell the outlaws infesting the state. Though the unpopular rebels after the war never enjoyed the veteran-love that most others received upon returning home, they did, on occasion, savor some revenge as outlaws.

Showdown-Shootout at Roscoe

Historic marker near Roscoe, Missouri, where the actual battle took place.

SHADES OF THE OLD, WILD WEST

Chronology

1819—Allan Pinkerton was born in Glasgow, Scotland.

1842—Allan Pinkerton moves to Chicago, Illinois.

1850—Allan Pinkerton establishes the Pinkerton National Detective Agency—their motto: "We never sleep."

January 31, 1874—The James-Younger Gang robs the train and station at Gads Hill, Missouri.

March 16, 1874—Pinkerton agents, Louis J. Lull and James Wright, along with Osceola Deputy Edwin B. Daniels, leave Osceola, Missouri, and head west towards Roscoe.

March 17, 1874—The lawmen are confronted by outlaws Jim and John Younger just north of Roscoe and a heated and deadly gunfight ensues.

Bibliography

Breihan, Carl W., *The Outlaw Brothers: The True Story of Missouri's Younger Brothers*, The Naylor Company, San Antonio, Texas, 1961.

Cimino, Al, *Gunfighters: A Chronicle of Dangerous Men and Violent Death*, Chartwell Books, New York, N.Y., 2016.

Funk & Wagnalls New Encyclopedia, Funk & Wagnalls, Inc., New York, 1979.

Jackson, Rex T., *Notable Persons and Places in Missouri's History*, The Ozarks Reader, Neosho, Missouri, 2006; *Monumental Tales from the Ozarks*, Heritage Books, Inc., Berwyn Heights, Maryland, 2015.

McNab, Chris, *Gunfighters: The Outlaws and Their Weapons*, Thunder Bay Press, San Diego, California, 2005.

Settle, Jr., William A., *Jesse James was His Name* or, *Fact and Fiction Concerning the Careers of the Notorious James Brothers of Missouri*, University of Nebraska Press, Lincoln, Nebraska, 1966.

Triplett, Frank, *Jesse James: The Life, Times, and Treacherous Death of the Most Infamous Outlaw of All Time*, Skyhorse Publishing, (reprint), 2013.

Wallis, Michael, *The Wild West 365*, Abrams, New York, N.Y., 2011.

Watts, Hamp B., *The Babe of the Company*, The Democrat-Leader Press, Fayette, Missouri, 1913.

Zinc, Wilbur, (article), St. Clair County Library, Osceola, Missouri.

Life and Times of Belle Starr

THE WILD WEST was a rugged time, even for the most determined man, but there were women who were as tough as nails that also shared in the difficulties of that time period. The era following the American Civil War spawned postwar anxiety, persecution, and bad blood. As a result, legendary outlaws began to roam and haunt the countryside. One of those female icons that rose out of the flames of that fiery past was Belle Starr—who, overtime, received these colorful sobriquets: "Outlaw Queen," "Bandit Queen," and "The Petticoat Terror" of the Old West.

It was during these turbulent times that John Shirley moved to southwest Missouri and settled about 10 miles northwest of Carthage near the small hamlet of Medoc. Shirley was born in Augusta County, Virginia, to a well-to-do family in 1796, and eventually after two failed unions married Elizabeth ("Eliza") Hatfield who was related to the Hatfield's of the now famous feuding Hatfield and McCoy families; however, some sources say Shirley's third wife's name was Eliza Pennington. While living in the northwestern part of Jasper County at Medoc, Eliza gave birth to Myra Maybelle Shirley on February 5, 1848. Myra later changed her middle name to "Bella" and usually signed this as a first name, but history, for the most part, remembers her as "Belle." Other Shirley children include: Edwin Benton, Charlotte A., John ("Bud") Allison, Mansfield, and Cravens.

After receiving a grant for 800 acres on June 30, 1848, for land

SHADES OF THE OLD, WILD WEST

Belle Starr is believed to have visited this brick, antebellum home of Matthew Ritchey (site of two significant Civil War battles) located in Newtonia, Missouri, during the war.

southeast of Medoc, Shirley prospered in farming—raising livestock and crops; however, in a few years he invested his resources in Carthage and dominated the north side of the downtown square, owning and operating the Shirley House Hotel and Tavern, a livery stable, and blacksmith shop.

Young Belle attended the Carthage Female Academy and studied and excelled in language—reportedly, besides English, she learned a fair amount of Greek, Latin, and Hebrew; mathematics; and music, especially the piano. Belle's brother, Bud Shirley, who was a strong influence on her, would join up with William Clarke Quantrill's Missouri raiders in support of the Southern cause during the Civil War. Belle would also become skilled with a variety of firearms and riding horses and began using those talents to spy for the Confederacy. In the summer of 1864, Belle's beloved brother Bud was gunned down by a Union soldier of the 15th Missouri Cavalry in Sarcoxie, Mo., while climbing over a fence trying to escape.

After the death of Bud and because of the increasing danger to Carthage and its tolerance of rebels, the Shirley's wisely abandoned southwest Missouri and headed south to the safety of Scyene, Texas, which was not far from Dallas. It was a smart exodus on their part because Federal troops taught Carthage a valuable lesson for their Southern tendencies and burned the town to the ground, including Shirley's once prosperous businesses.

It was at this time that a friend of Belle's, James ("Jim") C. Reed, who was also from Missouri and had been a former Confederate guerilla who had rode with Quantrill, began to court her; the two lovers tied the knot on November 1, 1866. And by late 1867, they had left Texas and were living on the Reed homestead at Rich Hill, Mo., where Belle gave birth to Rosie Lee. Soon after, Belle began referring to her as her "Pearl," and the nickname became permanent.

In no time at all, Belle's new husband was wanted by the law after murdering a man named Shannon who had accidentally shot and killed his younger brother, Scott Reed. As a result, they fled to Indian Territory (Oklahoma) and fell into bad company with "Old" Tom Starr, a Cherokee with a lawless reputation. However, before long they left their sanctuary in the Indian Nations and headed for

SHADES OF THE OLD, WILD WEST

California in early 1869. Belle gave birth to a son, James ("Ed") Edwin on February 22, 1871, while they were there. Trouble with the law would bring them back to the Shirley farm at Scyene that same year. Belle opened a gambling hall in Dallas and her husband continued his rampage—holding up stagecoaches and rustling livestock. Crime doesn't pay and Jim Reed was eventually shot through the heart by Deputy John T. Morris in Collins County.

After the death of her outlaw husband, and the death of her father in 1876, Belle left Texas and returned to Missouri and to the Reed home in Rich Hill. On June 5, 1880, Belle married Samuel ("Sam") Starr, a three-quarter Cherokee who was the son of Old Tom Starr. They made a claim on a large acreage on the Canadian River near present-day Porum, Oklahoma, which came to be known as "Younger's Bend," in honor of the lawless riff-raff that roamed the West. Younger's Bend soon became a gathering and stopping off place for outlaws, like Jesse James, the Younger brothers, and the Dalton Gang who sought refuge from the law at a trusted haven.

Things went well for a couple of years until a neighbor brought up charges of horse theft. After learning that Bass Reeves had put out an arrest warrant, Belle reportedly turned herself in; she and her husband were taken into custody at Younger's Bend. Reeves was a former slave who had gained a reputation of arresting and also killing a number of desperadoes while bringing them to justice. He served as one of Judge Isaac Parker's marshals for thirty-five years. Reeves died on January 12, 1910, at the age of seventy-two.

Isaac C. Parker was a devout Christian of the Methodist brand who came from St. Joseph, Missouri. He was [1] appointed by President Ulysses S. Grant to the Western District of Arkansas at Fort Smith in 1871, and for twenty-one years Judge Parker gained the infamous title of the "Hanging Judge." During his reign at the court he sentenced about 160 criminals to the gallows and heard at least 13,500 cases. His dungeons below the courthouse gained a ghastly reputation as the "Hell on the Border." The gallows, dubbed the "Gates of Hell," generally accommodated six ropes to complete the "awful enginery of death."

Judge Parker's famous executioner, George Maledon, who earned his own fame as the "Prince of Hangmen," was very proud

Reproduction gallows at the Fort Smith Historic Site in Fort Smith, Arkansas.

of his well-crafted nooses or "neckties" as they were sometimes referred to. Maledon fashioned his hanging ropes of hand-woven hemp, which were each lubricated with oil to prevent slippage. In all, the Prince of Hangmen successfully hung sixty condemned souls; he kept pictures of them on his workshop wall for the sake of remembrance.

After the Starr's were arrested, they were taken to Fort Smith to face Judge Parker. In 1883 Sam and Belle evaded Maledon's prized neckties and were sentenced to one year at the House of Corrections in Detroit, Michigan; however, after only nine months of incarceration they were paroled. It seems that Belle had gained favor with the warden in the Detroit lockup and, while she was there, she served as a secretary and an educational tutor to his children. After leaving Detroit they headed back to Indian Territory and their log cabin at Younger's Bend.

Belle would often spend time in nearby Fort Smith wearing velvet dresses adorned with her pearl handled pistols—and, while in town, she often went to Judge Parker's court to argue and plead for the rights of Native Americans and give legal advice to her beloved friend, Bluford ("Blue") Duck, who was a Cherokee facing murder charges. Rumor had it that Belle and Blue Duck were more than just friends.

The grim reaper would soon catch up to Sam Starr while attending a dance party in 1886. A posse member of the Cherokee Lighthorse Indian Police, Frank West, who had fired on Starr and his gang of ruffians several weeks before, recognized him at the party. West quickly drew his gun and, in the heated firefight, mortally wounded him; however, West was also killed in the exchange of gunfire.

Concerning the incident that led up to the fatal shooting of Sam Starr at the dance, the Little Rock *Gazette* reported on September 20, 1886, that "...Sam Starr, who has been dodging officers for several years, has been badly wounded in a conflict with Indian Police. Bella said her information was that police fired on and wounded Sam, killing his horse, without demanding his surrender and that fifty shots had been exchanged in the fight...."

By this time, newspaper articles and dime novels were making

Belle Starr

Belle Starr a household name. She reportedly took advantage of it and began making appearances at theaters, fair grounds, and other public events. Many thronged to see her in action, on horseback and firing her weapons with deadly precision.

Finally, in 1887 Belle married a Cherokee named Jim July; however, some sources say that he was a Creek Indian. Belle was somehow able to convince her new, young husband who was fifteen years younger than her, to change his name to Jim Starr.

On February 3, 1889, it would all come crashing down for Belle Starr, the Bandit Queen who gave sanctuary to infamous outlaws at Younger's Bend and had lived a life at odds with the law. She would be blown out of her saddle a couple of days before she turned forty-one. For the first time, though, Belle would not have to witness the death of her outlaw spouse, who was eventually shot as a horse thief by a U.S. deputy marshal in Indian Territory not long after her demise.

It was on a Sunday and Belle had stopped off at a neighbor's house after parting company from her husband. She visited with friends and had a bite to eat before riding out toward Younger's Bend. On a curve in the trail, Belle Starr was attacked by an unknown, determined assailant by a shotgun blast in the back. The back-shooting coward didn't stop there, as Belle tottered and fell from her saddle and onto the muddy roadbed, she was again shot in her face and neck to insure her lifeless fate.

Belle Starr, the now famous female outlaw of the Wild West, was buried in the front yard of her log cabin home at Younger's Bend near Porum, Oklahoma, with a pistol in her hand. Her marble headstone was engraved with thoughtful motifs—a bell, horse, and star which was bought and paid for by her daughter Pearl. An epitaph suitable to Belle's eventful life, read:

Belle Starr
Born in Carthage, Mo., Feb. 5, 1848,
Died, Feb. 3, 1889.

SHADES OF THE OLD, WILD WEST

> "Shed not for her the bitter tear
> Nor give the heart to vain regret,
> 'Tis but the casket that lies here,
> The gem that filled it sparkles yet."

Overtime, grave robbers and treasure hunters desecrated the burial site and surrounding area—but, no matter how much they dug, the legends of Belle Starr remained and only grew—of daring Confederate sympathies, spying, cattle rustling, horse thieving, robbery, murder and a host of other wild tales of the Old West. The era that brought forth such lawlessness will forever be marked by the short, but eventful life and times of Belle Starr.

Pearl Starr, who left such a heartfelt epitaph for her mother, went on to make a name for herself in nearby Fort Smith as a prostitute and madam. Through the latter part of the 1800s and early part of the 1900s, Pearl, also known as Belle's "Canadian Lily," would run a successful bordello in Fort Smith's red-light district. Playing off of her mother's fame and notoriety, Pearl, flaunting sexual freedom, banked much more than did her "respectable" female counterparts. In Fort Smith's "The Row," Pearl's Place offered beautiful women for pleasure—temporary companionship for the lonely.

Eventually, however, as times changed and Christian influence and opposition soared, the human flesh market waned in many areas of the United States. Later in life, Pearl packed her bags and headed for sunny Arizona where she died in the summer of 1925 in a hotel room. Chances are Pearl Starr probably never received a comparable epitaph in stone as did her beloved, outlaw mother.

Bibliography

Bearss, Edwin C., and Gibson, A.M., *Fort Smith: Little Gibraltar on the Arkansas*, University of Oklahoma Press, Norman, Oklahoma, 1969.

Breihan, Carl W., *Belle Starr: Oklahoma Whirlwind*, The West: True Stories of the Old West Magazine, Vol. 6, No., 4, Maverick Publications, Inc., Freeport, N.Y., 1967.

Enss, Chris, *More Tales Behind the Tombstones: More Deaths and Burials of the Old West's Most Nefarious Outlaws, Notorious Women, and Celebrated Lawmen*, Twodot, Guildford, Connecticut, 2015.

Jackson, Rex T., *Notable Persons and Places in Missouri's History*, The Ozarks Reader Regional Magazine, Litho Printers, Cassville, Missouri, 2006.

McLachlan, Sean, *Outlaw Tales of Missouri: True Stories of the Show Me State's Most Infamous Crooks, Culprits, and Cutthroats*, Twodot, Guildford, Connecticut, 2009.

Wallis, Michael, *The Wild West 365*, Abrams, New York, N.Y., 2011.

Wexler, Bruce, *How the Wild West was Won*, Skyhorse Publishing, New York, N.Y., 2013.

Other Sources:

St. Louis *Republican*, September 4, 1875.
Little Rock *Gazette*, September 20, 1886.

The Bloody Benders: Evil Along the Osage Trail

HOMESTEADERS and pioneers flocked to Kansas during the Western migration, and by the early part of the 1870s most of the best lands were already spoken for. By 1890, however, thanks to the Homestead Act, about 375,000 farms had been claimed. Two of these 160-acre tracks of land, which were located in present-day Labette County, Kansas, were claimed by a group known as the Benders. This diabolical family of misfits would go on to scar the state's history with unspeakable, haunting crimes of serial killing. Their land, which was located on the old Osage Trail where many souls traveled, would offer a perfect vantage ground for their profitable business of murder.

The Benders, made up and known as John ("Pa") Sr., "Ma", John Jr., and Kate, migrated to the area in 1871 as a family; though, it was never ascertained as to whether or not they were actually even related to each other. Right from the beginning, before the murders were even discovered, their acquaintances and neighbors were conjuring up cruel labels for them, like "satanic," "dim-witted," "she devil," or "witch." The Benders' misguided neighbors may have fallen into the old quagmire of hysteria, like the era of the "Witch Craze" or the "Burning Times" of the sixteenth or seventeenth century where about 40,000 people were executed. Visions of magic wands, potions, casting spells, broomsticks, black

SHADES OF THE OLD, WILD WEST

Monument to pioneers in Oswego, Kansas, about 30 miles southeast of Cherryvale.

The Bloody Benders

cats and pointy hats comes to the forefront of the mind. During the witch hunting period of 1692 in the New England hamlet of Salem, Massachusetts, 185 people suspected of witchcraft were accused, 59 were tried, and 20 were hanged by the neck; not to be forgotten or overlooked, however, is the 80-year-old farmer who was dragged out into a field where he was laid upon the earth with a wooden plank placed on his chest; and for two, long days heavy rocks were heartlessly stacked onto the plank until he was crushed to death on September 19, 1692, by his Christian neighbors.

Though the Kansans did not resort to witch trials, it may never be known as to whether or not their treatment or name-calling could have influenced or angered the Benders. In those times, there was not much known about mental illness and there were few treatments available—John Jr. was thought to be mentally challenged. Prejudice over other nationalities, religions, and beliefs other than Christianity, may have also played a role—Kate was known to be a believer in spiritualism.

When the Benders came to their land a few miles northeast of Cherryvale, they built a sixteen-by-twenty-foot one room framed cabin along the roadway with a small cellar beneath. In order to separate the business from their living quarters, they installed a large canvas to divide the space in half. In the front part the Benders created a type of store where they could offer foodstuff and supplies—the type of things that a wayward traveler might need; they also offered meals and a place to rest. Outside, they built a corral to hold livestock and dug a well as a source of water.

Pa, Ma, and John Jr. were said to speak with heavy German accents. Pa, reportedly, spent much of his spare time reading a German Bible, and John Jr. and Kate often attended Harmony Grove Church. Ironically, Kate, who was said to be very beautiful and easy on the eyes, claimed to be a medium and traveled around to nearby towns and conducted séances as "Professor Miss Kate Bender." She claimed she could speak to the dearly departed and heal the deaf, dumb, and blind. Strange that "locals", for the most part, believing in the resurrection of the dead and the Holy Ghost, would be judgmental of a spiritual person exercising her freedom of religion. Nevertheless, rumors began to blossom that she was a

SHADES OF THE OLD, WILD WEST

witch and talk of burning Kate alive was being discussed—the stage was now set.

As time went on and the Benders' popularity continued to tumble and plummet, people began to disappear. At first, it was thought that the lost souls might turn up, but when that failed to materialize and more and more were reported missing, fear began to set in. In the spring of 1873 almost 100 people of the local community, including Pa and John Jr., were summoned to a meeting at Harmony Grove Church to discuss the problem. As a result, they concluded that a search should be made in their immediate vicinity to see if they could find any clues or signs of the possible whereabouts of the ten or more people who were unaccounted for.

Not long after the "get together" it was discovered that the Benders' place appeared to be abandoned—their observation was correct, when their store-home was entered and searched they found that their worldly possessions were gone and they had vanished like smoke.

This is where it gets macabre and deserves at least a "restricted" rating. Even though the searchers failed to find the Benders—they did, however, smell a strange, unpleasant odor coming from the cellar. The space beneath the house was accessible through a trapdoor in the floor, which they soon opened. Down in its ghoulish bowels they discovered a large amount of mostly blood. A further, more exhaustive search in and under the structure turned up negative for bodies—either of the missing people or the Benders themselves.

The grounds, especially in the garden-orchard area, gave up the ghosts of the remains of about twelve of the missing—including a young girl who was apparently buried alive. Dismembered body parts were also uncovered and the crime scene was dubbed with names like "Hell's Acre" and "Hell's Half-Acre." It seemed like the locals could always come up with a clever label. In the end, it was believed that the Benders had victimized at least twenty people.

Beautiful Kate was the key, with her feminine wiles she was able to get and hold the intended victim's attention; they would then be seated at the meal table with their backs to the room-dividing-canvas. From behind the canvas, Pa or John Jr. would clobber the

The Bloody Benders

unsuspecting soul in the head with a sledgehammer. Afterwards, the victimized guest would be robbed of all their valuables and dropped into the cellar by the convenience of the trapdoor. Later on, at their discretion, they would retrieve the body and bury it outside in their secret cemetery.

As for the suspects, the searchers located some wagon-wheel tracks leading to Thayer, which is about twenty-five miles northeast of Cherryvale. The Benders, reportedly, then purchased train tickets, split into two separate groups, and headed in different directions never to be seen or heard of again. The governor of Kansas offered a five hundred dollar reward for each of the Benders, but to no avail.

Overtime, the Benders' homestead became a tourist destination where newspaper reporters, writers, souvenir hunters, and thousands of others descended—curiosity had obviously gotten the better of them. In 1889 the Benders' home and business was at long last razed. The rumors and stories continued to flow concerning the whereabouts of the family that may or may not have been related to one another. The "Bloody Benders" still, however, get labeled as history keeps remembering and trying to make sense of it all, with the hopes that someday understanding might prevail over evil. Over the years, passersby the old homestead site on the Osage Trail swear that they have seen ghosts and apparitions haunting the grounds. Possibly, the restless spirits only want to be remembered—or, they want to warn the living of their fates and for us to be extra careful and vigilant—or, maybe, they just want the living to be kind to one another.

SHADES OF THE OLD, WILD WEST

Chronology

Early 1870s—Most of the best lands had already been taken.
1890—About 375,000 farms had been claimed in Kansas due to the Homestead Act.

1870—John Sr. and John Jr. establish land claims in Labette County, Kansas.
1871—The Benders move to their new home in Kansas, including Ma and Kate.
1873—A community meeting is held about the disappearances of a number of individuals; and the Bender family homestead is suddenly abandoned.
1889—The Bender home is finally torn down.

Bibliography

Ballard, Jane, *The Bloody Benders*, Two Wheels, Four States Magazine, Vol. 1, No. 2, Joplin, Missouri, 2010.

Goldfield, David, *The American Journey: A History of the United States*, Prentice Hall, Upper Saddle River, New Jersey, 1998.

Martin, Lois, *The History of Witchcraft*, Chartwell Books, Inc., Edison, New Jersey, 2007.

Smith, Robert Barr, *Bad Blood: The Families Who Made the West Wild*, Twodot, Guilford, Connecticut, 2014.

Wallis, Michael, *The Wild West 365*, Abrams, New York, N.Y., 2011.

Calamity Jane: Teamster, Showgirl, Prostitute and Nurse

IN THE NORTHERN reaches of Missouri, about twenty-five miles north of Trenton and about thirteen miles south of the Iowa state line, is the small town of Princeton. Situated in the state's scenic, rolling farmlands and woodlands, Princeton is billed as the birthplace of Martha Jane Cannary—better known as "Calamity" Jane. This Missouri town had good reason to claim the strong, independent, legendary woman of America's Wild West. Her life in the frontier not only gave her the sobriquet Calamity, but also "Angel of Deadwood" and "Florence Nightingale"—a British nurse and humanitarian who gained her own nickname as the "Lady with the Lamp," because of the many vigil rounds she made in sick wards throughout the night.

Martha Jane Cannary was born on May 1, 1852, to James and Charlotte Cannary. When Martha was about twelve years old her family, including five siblings who were younger than her—four brothers and one sister, packed up and, leaving Princeton behind, headed west for the allure of the gold rush in Montana. The Cannary's arduous journey began at the end of the American Civil War, around 1865. They settled in the Virginia City area of Montana, but within a year or so both of her parents had passed away which left Calamity Jane in charge of her brothers and sister. With such a burden to bear, poor Calamity Jane had to grow up fast.

Illustration of Calamity Jane.

Calamity Jane

Around 1867 the brave teenager chose to take the brood to Fort Bridger, Wyoming, which is located in the southwestern corner of the state just west of Green River, where she did odd jobs to eke out a living—and, reportedly, stooped to prostitution. She eventually found homes for her brothers and sister, which allowed her a newfound freedom she'd never experienced before while in the Western wilds.

Calamity Jane went on to live a life as rough and brawny as any man, working side by side with them. She wore men's clothing and, for the most part, blended in and no one was the wiser. She drove freight wagons from Fort Bridger to Fort Laramie, which is clear across the state on the southeastern side. In her disguise as the rougher sex in order to get honest employment, she worked as a teamster and Indian tracker in 1876 with General George Crook, a United States army officer in the post-Civil War West on campaigns during the American Indian Wars. Her military days would soon come to an end, though, after meeting the love of her life, "Wild Bill" Hickok, and moving to Deadwood, South Dakota, in the busy year of 1876; however, Hickok always maintained that their relationship was only friendship and nothing more.

Deadwood, founded in April 1876, was a mining boomtown in the Black Hills of Dakota Territory at the confluence of the Whitewood and Deadwood rivers. In order to keep the riff-raff, which continued to pour in, happy, there were places to eat, hotels, stores, saloons, bordellos, gambling houses and so on, all hastily constructed of makeshift logs, canvas or what-have-you. The party never ceased, however, and money was won and lost—easy come, easy go, as the "placers" would squander their mining profits. The technique of mining, known as placers, is when a "miner takes his pick, shovel and pan and goes, sometimes all alone, digging and picking in the creeks and rivers. He [or she] lifts up a pan of sand and looks anxiously for the glistening grains of gold. He rinses and rinses the sand. By skillful dipping he finally gets all the sand out and has only the gold in the bottom of the pan. Sometimes he will find flakes as big as a pumpkin seed."

The town's twenty-yard-wide Main Street was always alive and bustling with the coming and going of the Cheyenne & Black Hills

Stagecoaches; and pioneering individuals on foot or by horse, buggy, ox-cart, or wagon, helped to keep Deadwood's thoroughfare full, as well. The hillsides at night would twinkle like the stars of many campfires and bonfires along the narrow canyon. Law and order, however, was lacking and at times fringed on all-out anarchy, similar to other lawless Western towns, like Abilene and El Paso, Texas; Dodge City, Kansas; and Tombstone, Arizona. One of Deadwood's main saloon areas became known as the "Badlands"— and for good reason, plagued by gunfights, intoxication, fist fights, arguments, gambling, prostitution and the list goes on—but, a perfect fit for the rugged likes of Wild Bill Hickok and Calamity Jane.

On August 2, 1876, a notorious gambler named Jack McCall who had a grudge against Wild Bill shot him in the back of the head at Deadwood's Number Ten Saloon. Calamity Jane was devastated at the loss of her friend. She attended the funeral of Wild Bill who was buried the next day at the Mount Moriah Cemetery in Deadwood on August 3, 1876. She grieved for months afterwards, but life went on as she continued working on her legend.

In 1878 a smallpox epidemic attacked Deadwood, and Calamity Jane sprang into action. She catered to the victims in town and across the plague-torn Dakotas as an angel of mercy—bringing medicines and cures at her own expense, encouraging the patients, and also helping to get many of the dead ready for burial.

Calamity Jane was making a name for herself in American history, and newspapers and dime novels were helping to make her a household name. In 1893 she joined "Buffalo Bill" Cody's Wild West Show riding and shooting her weapons. A new form of American entertainment was born which was championed by William Frederick Cody, a former buffalo hunter. It all began for Cody on July 4, 1882, with an event called "Old Glory Blowout." Cody's Scout's Rest Ranch, located near North Platte, Nebraska, hosted a rodeo-style hullabaloo involving about a thousand cowboys competing in lariat, bronco busting, shooting and other things pertinent to the West. The show served as a trial run for what was to come. Cody and Dr. W.F. Carver unveiled "The Wild West, Hon. W.F. Cody and Dr. W.F. Carver's Mountain and Prairie Exhibition"

Calamity Jane

on May 17, 1883, at the Omaha, Nebraska, fairgrounds; Calamity Jane joined the historic show ten years later.

Calamity Jane also participated in the Pan-American Exposition, which took place in Buffalo, New York, on September 6, 1901. The event was clouded, however, by the assassination of President William McKinley who was shot twice by an anarchist, Leon Czolgosz.

Over the years Calamity Jane had reportedly been married a few times and had, at least, one child—a daughter, which was placed in a convent and raised by Catholic nuns. In her final years, she became poor and homeless and found solace at the bottom of a liquor bottle. She began to wander around and wound up in Terry, South Dakota, and died there of pneumonia on August 1, 1903, while staying at the Callaway Hotel.

The remains of Calamity Jane were taken back to Deadwood and buried next to Wild Bill Hickok—at her request, at the Mount Moriah Cemetery. The eulogy was delivered by Seth Bullock, a friend of hers who was known as one of the fiercest advocates of law in all of Dakota's history. Bullock was born in Sandwich, Ontario, Canada, in 1847; in 1867 he moved to Montana; and by 1873 he was sheriff of Montana Territory. On August 1, 1876, Bullock relocated to Deadwood and proceeded to rid the streets of lawlessness.

The girl from Princeton that wound up in the Western frontier and soon found herself in dire straights, went on through hard times to make the best of it and carve out a place for herself at the table of American history. Her guts, bravery, independence, showmanship, generosity and so much more had served her well, and helped to make her humble Missouri birthplace a continued source of historical interest to future generations.

SHADES OF THE OLD, WILD WEST

Chronology

May 1, 1852—Martha Jane Cannary was born in Princeton, Missouri.

1867—Calamity Jane takes her brothers and sister to Fort Bridger, Wyoming, after the death of their parents.

1876—Calamity Jane serves as a teamster and Indian tracker for General George Crook; Deadwood, South Dakota, is founded in April; Calamity Jane moves to Deadwood—Wild Bill Hickok also moves there; Hickok is shot on August 2 by Jack McCall; Hickok is buried at the Mount Moriah Cemetery the next day.

May 17, 1883—Buffalo Bill's Wild West Show is established—Calamity Jane joins the show ten years later.

September 6, 1901—Calamity Jane participates in the Pan-American Exposition in Buffalo, New York.

August 1, 1903—Calamity Jane dies of pneumonia in Terry, South Dakota.

Calamity Jane

Bibliography

Bourke, John G., *On the Border with Crook: General George Crook, the American Indian Wars, and Life on the American Frontier*, Skyhorse Publishing, New York, N.Y., 2014.

Enss, Chris, *Love Lessons From the Old West: Wisdom From Wild Women*, Twodot, Guilford, Connecticut, 2014; *Tales Behind the Tombstones: The Deaths and Burials of the Old West's Most Nefarious Outlaws, Notorious Women, and Celebrated Lawmen*, Twodot, Guilford, Connecticut, 2007.

Funk & Wagnalls New Encyclopedia, Funk & Wagnalls, Inc., New York, N.Y., 1979.

George, Marian M., *Little Journeys to Alaska and Canada*, A. Flanagan Company, Chicago, Illinois, 1901.

Legrand, Jacques, *Chronicle of America*, Chronicle Publications, Inc., 1989.

McNab, Chris, *Gunfighters: The Outlaws and Their Weapons*, Thunder Bay Press, San Diego, California, 2005.

Morgan, Lael, *Wanton West: Madams, Money, Murder, and the Wild Women of Montana's Frontier*, Chicago Review Press, Inc., Chicago, Illinois, 2011.

Wallis, Michael, *The Wild West 365*, Abrams, New York, N.Y., 2011.

Tombstone:
Thirty Seconds
at the O.K. Corral

LONG BEFORE the Europeans had filtered into Arizona Territory in search of precious metals—like copper, silver, and gold, the region was inhabited by an indigenous race of Indians. They were an industrious group of people who were culturally advanced, leaving behind the ruins of their irrigation canals, aqueducts, fortifications, and dwelling-places as proof of their ancient, thriving civilization.

Later, in the nineteenth century, these same hills and canyons—littered with prickly pear cactus and greasewood shrubs, and highlighted by the Swisshelm, Dragoon, Pedregosa, Huachuas and other such mountains in the area, now bustled and crawled with miners, entrepreneurs, and settlers in the comfort of their adobe homes. The mining discoveries swelled towns overnight in population, but many times they decreased just as quickly when the mines petered out—commonly referred to as from boomtown to ghost town.

Along with all the hubbub and activity came lawlessness and the need for law and order. Many of the mining camps and cow towns that suffered from crime and violence were smart enough to adopt gun control laws which prohibited the carrying of handguns inside the city limits. Such unpopular restrictions offered employment to talented gunfighters as lawmen—men like "Wild Bill" Hickok and

SHADES OF THE OLD, WILD WEST

Illustrations from: *When a Man's a Man*, by Harold Bell Wright, A.L. Burt Company, New York, 1916.

Tombstone

Wyatt Earp. One such town of America's Wild West which enjoyed its share of all these things, was Tombstone, Arizona, located in the southeast corner of the state; Tucson is about sixty miles to the northwest.

In 1877 a man by the name of Ed Schieffelin, who was doing a bit of prospecting in Arizona Territory near Camp Huachuca, discovered a vein of silver and dubbed his mining claim "Tombstone." At the time, the region was a dangerous place for trespassers in Apache lands, and Schieffelin may have considered these deadly possibilities when naming his claim. In spite of it all, Tombstone was laid out a couple of years later and had blossomed to about one thousand strong by 1881. Over 100 different businesses were created in a short time to cater to the ever increasing multitudes.

With all the goings-on in Tombstone, the lawmen were probably outmanned and outgunned. Sheriff John Behan had his plate full, but there were others on hand to share the load, like town marshal Virgil Earp, and his deputy and brother, Morgan; another "ace in the hole" was deputy Untied States marshal Wyatt Earp—yet another family lawman. However, Sheriff Behan and the Earps were not the best of friends, for some reason, even though they were on the same side.

Wyatt Berry Stapp Earp, the most well-known of the group, was born in Monmouth, Illinois, on March 19, 1848, to Nicholas Porter Earp and Virginia Anne Earp. While there, Nicholas served as a volunteer deputy in that lawless region of western Illinois, which may have inspired Wyatt's future employment tendency toward law enforcement; and the other Earp boys, as well.

The Earps moved to Pella, Iowa, and when the American Civil War began Nicholas served as a captain and provost marshal in Marion County for the Union—recruiting and drilling troops. While Wyatt's elder brothers were off fighting in the War Between the States, he stayed home and worked on the farm. By 1869, the Earp family traveled to southwest Missouri and settled in Lamar—the birthplace of President Harry S. Truman. Nicholas became the Lamar town constable but resigned on November 17, 1869, to become the Justice of the Peace.

SHADES OF THE OLD, WILD WEST

Above: Entrance to the Howell Cemetery just south of Milford, Missouri; Below: Gravesite of Urilla Earp–wife of Wyatt Earp.

A few weeks later, Wyatt Earp would wed Urilla Southerland on January 10, 1870. Wyatt Earp would pin on a badge for the first time at the age of twenty-one on March 3, 1870, as constable of Lamar.

Wyatt's life with Urilla was short-lived—Urilla would die several months after they were married, either of typhoid or childbirth. She is buried in Barton County a few miles northeast of Lamar at the Howell Cemetery—or, just south of the hamlet of Milford. In November 1870, Wyatt sold the home that they had bought together and soon afterwards he left Lamar behind.

Wyatt Earp would go on to be married three times and befriend famous historical figures, like Ed and Bat Masterson—and, of course, "Doc" Holliday. He would also serve as a deputy marshal in Wichita and Dodge City, Kansas, and deputy United States marshal while in Tombstone, Arizona. Wyatt Earp died on January 13, 1929, in Los Angeles, California, at the ripe old age of eighty.

Doc Holliday, a gunslinger that enjoyed the heyday of Tombstone by way of Dodge City, Kansas, and Tucson, was born John Henry Holliday on August 14, 1851, in Griffin, Georgia, to Henry Burroughs Holliday and Alice Jane (McKey) Holliday. His father served in the Confederate army as a major and later became the Mayor of Valdosa, Georgia, located in the extreme south-central part of the state. Doc attended a dental college in Pennsylvania and was later diagnosed with tuberculosis after his health began to fail. He was told that a drier climate might help him to live a longer life. In Dodge City he opened up a dental clinic and advertised his business in the Dodge City *Times* on June 8, 1878, to offer his services to the public, saying:

"Dentistry
J.H. Holliday, Dentist, very respect-
fully offers his professional services to the
citizens of Dodge City and surrounding
country during the summer. Office at
room No. 24, Dodge House. Where sat-
isfaction is not given money will be re-
funded."

SHADES OF THE OLD, WILD WEST

Mural depicting Wyatt Earp in the Barton County Courthouse in Lamar, Missouri.

While Doc Holliday had his practice in Dodge City he met and befriended Wyatt Earp—and, reportedly, may have saved his life on at least one occasion during an altercation at the town's Long Branch Saloon. It is a well-known fact that Doc Holliday had a reputation of being ambidextrous and a lightning fast, quick draw with his guns. During his time in the Old West, like many of his type, he was, at times, believed to be at odds with the law. Holliday eventually succumbs to tuberculosis at a sanitarium in Glenwood Springs, Colorado, on November 8, 1887, and was laid to rest at the Linwood Cemetery. But before all of that occurred, when Wyatt Earp and his band of brothers decided to leave Dodge City and head for Tombstone, Doc Holliday, probably thinking that it might be an even better place for his health and wanting to continue being near the Earps, joined them in the Arizona boomtown.

In the midst of all the gambling, liquor, and women were the miners and the cowboys who frequented the popular places in town, like the Oriental Saloon and the Crystal Palace. Numbered among them were the Clantons, a family of crooked cowpokes who were feuding with the Earps.

The patriarch of the outlaw family was Newman Haynes Clanton, or better known as "Old Man" Clanton, who was born in Tennessee in 1816. Old Man Clanton eventually put down roots in Missouri, and out of his brood of five sons three were born in the state; he also had a couple of daughters too. He served in the Civil War and later relocated to the Tombstone area.

A rash of cattle rustling was attributed to the Clanton gang, mostly perpetrated upon Mexican herds, which might explain why Old Man Clanton was eventually shot and killed on August 13, 1881, while he was asleep—encamped in Guadalupe Canyon.

The conundrum came to a head after Virgil and Morgan Earp had confiscated Joseph Isiah ("Ike") Clanton's gun and knocked him to the ground. Another occurrence that exacerbated the situation was when Wyatt pistol-whipped Tom McLaury—the McLaurys were comrades of the Clantons. A decision was made by the Earps to confront and arrest the Clanton gang who were in town. Sheriff Behan, after learning about the heated exchanges between the feuding parties and surmising that a confrontation was probably inevitable, headed for the O.K. Corral, Livery and Feed Stables where the outlaws were—to warn them to leave town as soon as possible and to try and convince them to disarm.

When Sheriff Behan reached the O.K. Corral he found Ike and Billy Clanton, Thomas ("Tom") and William Roland ("Frank") McLaury, and last but not least, William C. ("Billy") Claiborne. It was nearing three o'clock in the afternoon on October 26, 1881, as a deputized force of four, Virgil, Morgan, and Wyatt Earp, along with Doc Holliday, were "loaded for bear" and headed their way. Virgil and Morgan were packing .45 Colt "Peacemakers" and Wyatt was armed with a .44 Smith & Wesson New Model No. 3 American, while Doc sported a sawed-off Meteor 10 gauge shotgun he had affectionately dubbed his "street howitzer"—for close encounters.

Outside of the O.K. Corral on Fremont Street in front of Fly's Lodging House and Gallery, is where the determined lawmen had tracked down their quarry—Ike and Billy Clanton, Tom and Frank McLaury, and Billy Claiborne. The law, walking side by side down the south side of Fremont Street near the Tombstone Post Office, could see the hated outlaws coming closer into their view. Somewhere, near the Bauer's Butcher Shop, Sheriff Behan approached the deputies and tried to avert the coming disaster—but, to no avail.

When the lawmen reached the Clanton gang outside the O.K. Corral preparing to saddle up and hightail it out of town, they confronted them then and there and were ready for a heated showdown. As they eyeballed each other "at daggers drawn," Wyatt taunted the gang and said: "You S.O.B.'s, you've been looking for a fight and now you can have it."

Suddenly, two shots rang out simultaneously as Wyatt fired on Frank McLaury and Billy Clanton opened up on Wyatt. Frank was gut shot, and as more bullets were unleashed, Morgan hit Billy in his right wrist and chest. While all of this was going on, Holliday was blasting away with his double-barrel street howitzer hitting Tom McLaury squarely—both Billy and the two McLaury brothers died in agony. When the black powder dissipated and it was all said and done, they discovered that Ike Clanton and Billy Claiborne had somehow escaped unscathed.

Tombstone

The Battle of the O.K. Corral lasted for thirty long seconds, and in that half minute, it seared and secured an enduring place in America's Wild West history. The deadly conflict has been immortalized in many newspaper articles, magazine features, books, television shows and movies, all attempting to glean from the historical event the truth about lawlessness and order, and rules and anarchy.

SHADES OF THE OLD, WILD WEST

Chronology

March 19, 1848—Wyatt Berry Stapp Earp is born in Monmouth, Illinois.

August 14, 1851—John Henry ("Doc") Holliday is born in Griffin, Georgia.

1869—The Earp family moves to Lamar, Missouri.

January 10, 1870—Wyatt weds Urilla Southerland in Lamar.

March 3, 1870—Wyatt become constable of Lamar.

November 1870—After the untimely death of Urilla, Wyatt leaves Lamar.

1877—Ed Schieffelin discovers silver and calls his claim "Tombstone."

1879—The town of Tombstone is laid out.

1881—There is already 1,000 people in Tombstone.

October 26, 1881—The Battle at the O.K. Corral occurs.

November 8, 1887—Doc Holliday dies in Glenwood, Colorado.

January 13, 1929—Wyatt Earp dies in Los Angeles, California.

Bibliography

Funk & Wagnalls New Encyclopedia, Funk & Wagnalls, Inc., New York, 1979.

Goldfield, David, *The American Journey: A History of the United States*, Prentice Hall, Upper Saddle River, New Jersey, 1998.

Jackson, Rex T., *Notable Persons and Places in Missouri's History*, The Ozarks Reader, Neosho, Missouri, 2006.

Legrand, Jacques, *Chronicle of America*, Chronicle Publications, Inc., Mount Kisco, New York, 1989.

McNab, Chris, *Gunfighters: The Outlaws and Their Weapons*, Thunder Bay Press, San Diego, California, 2005.

Raine, William MacLeod, *Famous Sheriffs and Western Outlaws: Incredible True Stories of Wild West Showdowns and Frontier Justice*, Skyhorse Publishing, New York, N.Y., 2012.

Roark, James L., *The American Promise: A History of the United States*, Bedford Books, Boston, 1998.

Turner, George, *Gun Fighters*, L. Baxter Lane Publisher, Amarillo, Texas, 1972.

Wallis, Michael, *The Wild West 365*, Abrams, New York, N.Y., 2011.

Chief Black Kettle and the Slaughters at Sand Creek and Washita

WITH THE battle cry of "Manifest Destiny," western expansion of a beautiful America and all of its valuable resources, was too much of an irresistible temptation to ignore—but, to obtain these avarice treasures there were many obstacles and complications which needed to be solved. One of these problems was addressed in 1867 by the commissioner of the Indian Bureau, who offered this frustrated view and opinion concerning one of the biggest roadblocks that obstructed the way forward for westward migration, saying that it had "cost the government over $40,000,000 to conduct the campaign of 1865; and that at the present rate of extermination [genocide] it would take twenty-five thousand years, at a cost of $300,000,000,000 to be rid of the 'red fiends.'"

In order for the whites to possess all of America's wonders, many believed that its indigenous inhabitants would have to be relocated, converted through Christianization, or exterminated. To do this, civilized behavior, in many cases, was conveniently forsaken as a means to an end. As Native Americans continued to lose precious ground, confrontations and attacks became more frequent, violent, and ghastly—on both sides.

In southeastern Colorado a peaceful group of Cheyenne and Arapaho, under chief's Black Kettle (Moketaveto) and White Antelope, were camped along Sand Creek on land known as the

SHADES OF THE OLD, WILD WEST

Sand Creek Reservation about forty miles from Fort Lyon. The tribes had no reason to fear, since the United States government had recently guaranteed and promised them safety and protection. Whether or not this was a clever ploy to lull them into blind trust is unknown. While the Civil War raged in the East, a different type of genocidal war was horrifyingly unfolding in the West; in this case, Colorado Territory. The work of genocide, though, drew such little national outrage that it went, in the end, unpunished and conveniently tolerated.

On a chilly morning, just as our faithful star was beginning to peek out above the eastern horizon, on November 29, 1864, while about six hundred Native Americans slept along Sand Creek, cuddled together—mostly women, children, and old people, a wild-for-blood detachment of about six hundred and fifty soldiers descended upon them. The regiments of the First and Third Colorado Cavalry, made up of a blood-thirty gang of barroom ruffians and other volunteer lowlifes, was led by Colonel John Milton Chivington, a Christian, Methodist minister and "circuit rider" some called the "Fighting Parson." These "wolves in sheep's clothing" were armed, though, with death-dealing mountain howitzers and rifles, and they had anything but "love thy neighbor" on their hearts and minds. Colonel Chivington had visions of greatness, grandeur, and personal gain on his agenda, to help his political aspirations—but, mostly, to satisfy the hatred of Indians that permeated his immoral soul. To make matters worse, the leader of the camp was Chief Black Kettle, a man of peace and accommodation who had already previously surrendered; and flapping proudly in the November breeze above the Indian village was America's "Stars and Stripes"—and also a white flag of truce.

It made little or no difference to Chivington's faithful flock of hypocrites bent on killing the heathens. As the First and Third Colorado Cavalry rode down hard upon the unsuspecting, slumbering camp, with guns blazing, more than two hundred souls were taken without mercy or warning—they were assaulted, scalped, brained, mutilated, and gutted. The proud troops adorned their hats and saddles with grisly souvenirs and saved a hundred or more Indian scalps as proof of their ungodly crimes. Later on, the

Chief Black Kettle

private scrotums of Indian braves were tanned like animal hides and fashioned into tobacco pouches for use in their smoking pipes; and purses were later made of the pudendum of Cheyenne women. The Fighting Parson went home and was received as a military, war hero. He traveled around and made public appearances on stage and reminisced about his genocidal, American atrocity and showed off his many Sand Creek scalps to loyal, deplorable audiences— proudly continuing to defend his cowardly slaughter of defenseless Cheyenne and Arapaho women and children.

Somehow, Chief Black Kettle and his wife managed to survive the massacre; however, Black Kettle's wife had received nine gunshot wounds and was in critical condition. In order to save her fading life, Black Kettle carried her all the way to Fort Lyon. The other survivors, having learned from their white brethren how to do it, went on a series of their own killing sprees in retaliation through parts of Kansas, Nebraska, Wyoming, and Colorado. This probably made the Indians "fair game" to the delight of many Manifest Destiny expansionists.

Col. Chivington, founder of Denver's first Sunday school, faced investigation and the news media made an attempt to condemn the barbarism; however, no charges were ever filed against the fire and brimstone Christian preacher. For Chief Black Kettle and his wife, as well as other tribe members, the road ahead would not be long.

On behalf of his people, Black Kettle signed the Little Arkansas Treaty in 1865 and the Medicine Lodge Treaty in 1867—always trying to keep the young braves peaceful and protecting the Southern Cheyenne from harm. To further this endeavor, Chief Black Kettle and Chief Big Mouth of the Arapaho, went on a mission to Fort Cobb in Oklahoma Indian Territory in November 1868 to persuade General William B. Hazen to guarantee the safety of his people. Gen. Hazen told Black Kettle and Big Mouth that only General Philip Henry Sheridan or Lieutenant Colonel (Brevet Major General) George Armstrong Custer had the authority to fulfill such a request. As a result, having done their best to protect the lives of their people, Black Kettle and Big Mouth, failing in their attempt, returned to their villages on the Washita River. Unbeknownst to the chiefs, deadly plans were already being hatched by the United States

SHADES OF THE OLD, WILD WEST

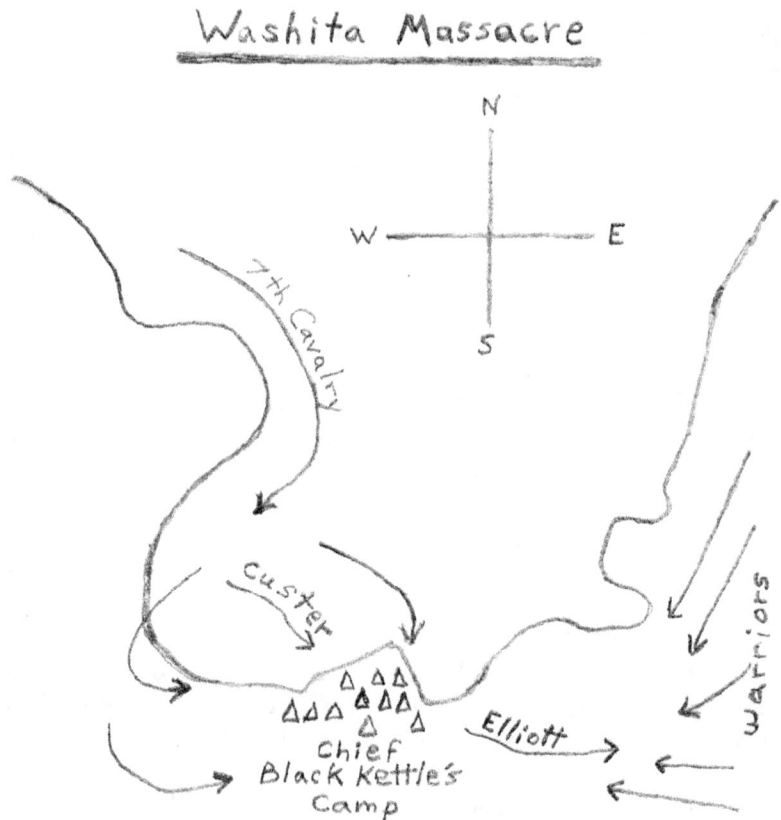

Illustration showing the Washita Massacre which occurred in western Oklahoma Indian Territory on November 27, 1868.

Chief Black Kettle

military that would go on to leave a permanent stain on American history.

Dubbed "The Boy General" by the news media, George Armstrong Custer attended West Point and finished dead last in a class of thirty-four cadets. During the American Civil War, his pluck and dash on the battlegrounds caught the watchful eyes of his superiors and he was catapulted to brigadier general by the tender age of twenty-three, which made him the youngest soldier to achieve such a rank in the Union army during the War of the Rebellion. In 1874, Custer's book about his time with the Seventh Cavalry, *My Life on the Plains*, was published; however, it was first seen in a periodical called *The Galaxy* starting in 1872. In it, Custer expressed his views about Native Americans and said that after they made raids on white settlements they forfeited their innocent title and were nothing more than savages, and compared them to wild beasts.

Under orders from General Sheridan, Lt. Col. Custer and his Seventh Cavalry, numbering about eight hundred, left Camp Supply on November 23, 1868. Camp Supply, located in northwestern Oklahoma at the mouth of the Cherokee Strip, was established as a base of operations and served as an ammunition magazine. Its walls were made ten-feet high which contained a couple of storehouses for supplies. The fortification had two blockhouses, one on one end and one on the other. Earthworks and huts accommodated and protected troops.

During Custer's march south toward Black Kettle's village on the Washita River, which was about seventy-five miles distance, a blizzard-like snowstorm began to fall, which continued until it reached about a foot in depth. Custer's plan was to attack at dawn.

On November 26, 1868, Lt. Col. Custer, or "Long Hair" as the Indians liked to call him, divided his forces into four detachments, leaving his baggage train near Antelope Hills which was on the Canadian River, and posted his army so that Black Kettle's village was completely surrounded. Custer's men lingered throughout the bitter, winter night until the wee morning hours of November 27, 1868. The army sprang into action with the sound of bugles and the regimental band playing the popular song *Garryowen*, an old Irish drinking or marching song which first emerged in the late 1700s. The song's Gaelic meaning "Eoins" and "garra" translates to: "Johnny's Garden." The song's Irish roots are traced to County Limerick, Ireland, which is located in the fertile farming plains of north Munster where some of the agricultural practices date back to Neolithic times. The city of Limerick is at the head waters of the Shannon Estuary. Musically, the word limerick is explained as a light or humorous five-line rhyming verse which was first found in Great Britain in the early 1800s, where Edward Lear's work helped to make it famous.

Even though Custer had planned for the old Irish tune played by the regiment's bandsmen, be the signal for the bloody attack to commence, a gunshot from the direction of Black Kettle's camp may have actually been the massacre's trigger. The Seventh Cavalry charged pell-mell into the sleeping, unprepared Indian encampment firing their weapons—it became a slaughter-house of death.

The foredoomed Cheyenne and Arapaho sprang from their lodges to face the onslaught of crazed troopers bearing down upon them. Many of the people were nearly naked and were helpless; Black Kettle and his wife would not be as fortunate as they had been at Sand Creek, they fell, shot in the back; others ran for the river and died in the icy confines of the blood-soaked waters; while the whole camp became littered with a mass of dead and dying bodies strewn throughout the snow-covered grounds which was now turned blood-red; finally, the lodges were burned to the ground and the camp looted. There were trampled children and victims of souvenir-scalping to showcase and spotlight the white man's need for revenge-killing. Weapons, ammunition, and a winter's supply of buffalo meat meant to sustain the tribe through the long winter's months, was also put to the flame.

By the time their fellow Indians who were camped nearby heard the commotion and responded, Custer and his army had turned-tail and skedaddled, retreating to safety. Left behind to rot in the snow were over 100 men, women, and children—and over 700 Indian ponies with their throats cut. Most of the casualties, about twenty, that were suffered by the Seventh Cavalry, happened to the east of the camp, belonging to Major Joel Elliot's command; they were killed by Cheyenne, Arapaho, and Kiowa braves coming to offer assistance to their neighbor. One of the soldiers who died that historic day was the grandson of Alexander Hamilton—his name was Captain Lewis M. Hamilton.

About the atrocities committed at Washita, a number of Americans cried foul while others thought that the massacre was justified. In the East some labeled the United States military cowards who attacked sleeping Indian villages and even stooped to murdering innocent, swaddled babies. Others, however, less concerned about crimes against humanity, felt that Indians should be exterminated.

Custer's work that day at Washita earned him a great deal of fame as an Indian fighter, which probably helped to lead the way to his participation at the upcoming battle at the Little Bighorn. As Long Hair was leaving Fort Abraham Lincoln in Dakota Territory with the Seventh Cavalry heading for their own massacre, once again his regimental band was playing *The Girl I Left Behind*—and, of course, the Irish song from Limerick: *Garryowen*.

As white America, for the most part, embraced Manifest Destiny and western conquest, it also tolerated, planned, and executed the extermination of America's indigenous inhabitants. On the other hand, Chief Black Kettle left his mark in American history as a peace-loving Native American leader, who somehow escaped the horrors of Sand Creek but was shot in the back not long afterwards by the United States army at Washita in Indian Territory.

Chronology

November 29, 1864—Massacre at Sand Creek.

November 23, 1868—Custer and the Seventh Cavalry leave Camp Supply on their way to Washita.

November 26, 1868—Custer divides his forces into four detachments and surrounds Black Kettle's camp.

November 27, 1868—Custer attacks Chief Black Kettle's camp on the Washita River in western Oklahoma Indian Territory in the wee hours of the morning while they slept.

Bibliography

Custer, George A., *My Life on the Plains*, University of Nebraska Press, Lincoln, Nebraska, 1966.

Jackson, Rex T., *Timeless Stories of the West: Mountaineers, Miners, and Indians*, Heritage Books, Inc., Berwyn Heights, Maryland, 2016.

Lalor, Brian, *The Encyclopedia of Ireland*, Yale University Press, New Haven and London, 2003.

Legrand, Jacques, *Chronicle of America*, Chronicle Publications, Inc., Mount Kisco, New York, 1989.

Mayo, Matthew P., *Hornswogglers, Fourflushers, & Snake-Oil Salesmen*, Twodot, Guilford, Connecticut, 2015.

McReynolds, Edwin C., *Oklahoma: A History of the Sooner State*, University of Oklahoma Press, Norman, 1954.

Muzzey, David Saville, *The United States of America: II From the Civil War*, Ginn and Company, Boston, 1924.

Noyes, C. Lee, *A Tale of Two Battles: George Armstrong Custer and the Attacks at the Washita and Little Bighorn*, Journal of the Indian Wars, Vol. 1, No. 1, Savas Publishing Company, Mason City, Iowa, 1999.

Rea, Bob, *Sheridan & Custer: Camp Supply and the Winter Campaign of 1868-1869*, Journal of the Indian Wars, Vol. 1, No. 1, Savas Publishing Company, Mason City, Iowa, 1999.

Sides, Hampton, *Blood and Thunder: The Epic Story of Kit Carson and the Conquest of the American West*, Anchor Books, New York, 2006.

Wallis, Michael, *The Wild West 365*, Abrams, New York, N.Y., 2011.

Wellman, Paul I., *Death on Horseback: Seventy Years of War for the American West*, J.B. Lippincott Company, New York, 1947.

The Long Walk and the Navajo Exodus

IN THE East the decimation and relocation of Native Americans gave the Untied States much of its first land-grabbing victories. One of the most well-known of these happened to the Cherokee people who feared genocide. On December 29, 1835, by the flickering candlelight and glow of a hearth's fire, in Elias Boudinot's crowded house in the old Cherokee capital of New Echota, Georgia, the Treaty of New Echota was signed. The treaty ceded to the United States the entire Cherokee Nation lands east of the Mississippi River. The act would eventually spawn a historical journey westward that would be appropriately called the Cherokee "Trail of Tears," or "trail where we cried." The cruel march harvested over 4,000 human lives before they had reached Oklahoma Indian Territory—mostly women, children, and old people.

In 1845, a newspaper man who supported the annexation of Texas wrote about it in the July-August edition of the *United States Magazine and Democratic Review*, a periodical he helped to establish. O'Sullivan coned the popular catch phrase with religious overtones, "Manifest Destiny," in the magazine, saying that it was "Manifest Destiny to overspread the continent"—and, basically, that the territorial expansion of the nation was ordained by God. Between 1845 and 1848, a Christian crusade of western conquest expanded the United States about 70 percent in size and Anglos dominated the North American continent.

Much like the forced Indian relocations from the East to the

SHADES OF THE OLD, WILD WEST

West, there were similar treks which removed tribes from the American Southwest, and forced them eastward to New Mexico Territory. In 1862 while the American Civil War was being fought, General James Henry Carleton, who was the newly appointed United States commander of the territory, decided it was time to take action concerning the Indian population. In order to deal with the situation, General Carleton turned to "Kit" Carson.

Christopher Carson was born in Madison County, Kentucky in 1809, but when he was one year old he relocated to Missouri and grew up in the hamlet of Franklin in the "Boone's Lick Country" along the Missouri River. He became an apprentice to a saddle maker but yearned to go west, so he joined a Santa Fe caravan bound for Santa Fe, New Mexico Territory. Throughout his eventful lifetime, Carson served as a scout, trapper, hunter, and also waged campaigns against Native Americans in the American Southwest— the Apaches, Comanches, Kiowas, and Navajo. During the Navajo War, Carson became known as the "eyes of the cavalry."

Gen. Carleton sent Kit Carson and his army of New Mexico Volunteers into Mescalero Apache country to attack, decimate and kill as many warriors as possible. By January 1863, Carson and his troops had demoralized the tribe and had captured about 450 Apaches, which they escorted about 130 miles back to New Mexico and Bosque Redondo, close to an old trading post; a new adobe fortification called Fort Sumner was also constructed in the area. The fort was on the Pecos River in east-central New Mexico about 120 miles southeast of Santa Fe. The old town of Santa Fe, on the Santa Fe Trail, was founded in 1609.

After Carson had accomplished this, he headed back west to make war on the Navajo people. The word Navajo means "people with big lands" in Spanish, while the Navajos called themselves the "Dine," or simply the "people." Carson's attack on the Navajos was merciless, and before long they were whipped into submission. Before the end of 1864, Carson and his army of Indian killers were herding about ten thousand broken and starving prisoners on a grueling, 450-mile forced march back to New Mexico Territory to join the small group of Apaches already at Bosque Redondo.

The long procession stretched for miles as they marched to the

The Long Walk

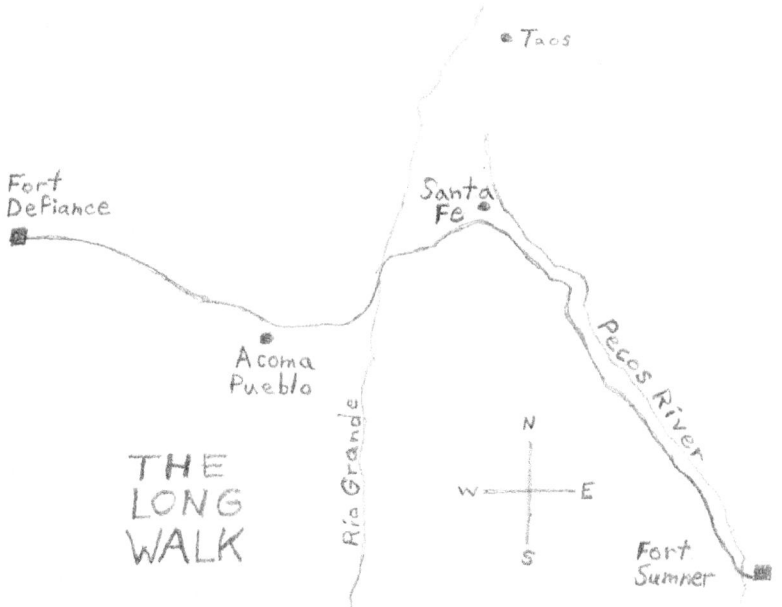

Illustration of the path taken on the Navajo's "Long Walk."

east, past such places like Acoma Pueblo and Laguna Pueblo, and along the Rio Grande and Pecos rivers. Many of the Navajo who fell along the way were weak and in poor health, exhausted, abused, and starving because the food rations were inadequate. The treatment of the Navajo people was anything but kind or Christian-like—something the military had promised. The marchers that could not keep up the pace were shot at close range and left to rot along the trail—even pregnant women. Soldiers, seizing an easy opportunity to sexually assault a vulnerable female, raped them. The "Long Walk" took the lives of many of the helpless marchers before reaching Bosque Redondo and the Pecos River Valley. Much like the Cherokee Trail of Tears, that continues to cry out for further remembrance and outrage, the Navajo Long Walk and its estimated five hundred lost souls, weeps also. The death toll didn't stop there, in the next few years about a quarter of the tribe had perished to sickness or starvation.

The Arapaho's and Navajo's new reservation-home at Bosque Redondo did not go well. Gen. Carleton built them a Christian church and a school and attempted to convert and Christianize them, but they could not understand why they had to give up their freedom in the land of the free to become slaves to the Anglo-American way and interpretations. They wondered why the whites worked day and night to build giant homes and businesses, and then when they died they had to leave it all behind. Ironically, after all the horrors and loss of life as a result of Kit Carson's attacks upon them; the ungodly experiences on the Long Walk; and the time spent being converted and brainwashed at Bosque Redondo Reservation; the Untied States War Department eventually had a change of heart in 1868 and decided that they would, like the Israelites' exodus from Egypt—as the story goes, let the people go. Peace was declared and the Navajo were released from the reservation-prison and allowed to return to their homeland.

Bibliography

Athearn, Robert G., *American Heritage New Illustrated History of the United States*, Vol. 6, *The Frontier*, Fawcett Publications, Inc., One Astor Plaza, New York, N.Y., 1963.
Jackson, Rex T., *Timeless Stories of the West: Mountaineers, Miners, and Indians*, Heritage Books, Inc., Berwyn Heights, Maryland, 2016; *A Trail of Tears: The American Indian in the Civil War*, Heritage Books, Inc., Westminster, Maryland, 2004; *Boone's Lick Country and the Life and Times of Kit Carson*, The Ozarks Reader Magazine, Neosho, Missouri, 2010.
Legrand, Jacques, *Chronicle of America*, Chronicle Publications, Inc., Mount Kisco, New York, 1989.
Sides, Hampton, *Blood and Thunder: The Epic Story of Kit Carson and the Conquest of the American West*, Anchor Books, New York, 2006.
Wallis, Michael, *The Wild West 365*, Abrams, New York, N.Y., 2011.
Wexler, Bruce, *How the Wild West was Won*, Skyhorse Publishing, New York, 2013.

Pacific Railroad Disaster: Engine of Western Conquest

THE WORK of "overspreading" the nation depended upon many things, but technology was a key component. A new invention that was gaining traction was the steam-powered locomotive. The first railway to carry passengers was England's "Stockton & Darlington," which traveled about twelve miles; it began on September 27, 1825, and successfully transported not only excursionists, but some freight.

America must have been impressed, two years later in 1827 a railway was laid from Quincy, Massachusetts, to Boston—about ten miles, which hauled granite to construct the Bunker Hill Monument. However, it wasn't until August 1829 that America had used a locomotive to carry passengers; the engine was shipped from England to the Delaware & Hudson Canal Company and used near Honesdale, Pennsylvania, and dubbed the "Stourbridge Lion."

Early passenger cars were crude, and those who rode in them were stuffed into narrow, uncomfortable seats. In winter, the cars had a heating stove at each end, which cooked passengers who were seated near them while those in the center of the car nearly froze to death. Lighting was provided by candle power, which was dim and filled the car with the smell of burning wax. The car's windows allowed the engine's smoke and soot to invade the train's interior, and by the time the passengers had reached their destination, they were blackened.

Help was on the way; in 1867 George M. Pullman established

DAILY M

TERRIBLE CATASTROPHE!

The Excursion Cars to Jefferson City precipitated into the Gasconade River!

Probable Death of many of our Distinguished Citizens!!

Last evening about 8 o'clock, we received the terrible information, through Mr. David H. Bishop and William Rumbold, citizens of this place, that the excursion train of twelve or fourteen cars, that departed from St. Louis yes-

Headlines from the St. Louis *Daily Missouri Democrat*, November 2, 1855.

Pacific Railroad Disaster

the Pullman Car Company and began producing a more luxurious passenger car. Eventually, cars like the parlor or drawing-room were utilized and came to be known as "palace cars"—in time, passengers would even enjoy sleeping cars for long journeys.

The railroads continued to expand and grow, and by the 1850s there was already about 2,160 miles of track being laid per year; by 1870 the amount of rails in the eastern United States had blossomed to about fifty-three thousand miles. With the nation's population exploding from 12.8 million in 1830 to about 31 million in 1860, the vastness of the American West was an irresistible temptation, and the railroad was a perfect way to get there.

In order to cross certain places, bridges needed to be built. At first, bridges were constructed of wood and were known as trestle bridges. By 1888 it was estimated that there was already 147,187 wooden trestle bridges in the United States. However, there was danger involved with these type of bridges—decay, fire, and possible weakness. As time went on, however, wood gave way to iron and steel. The failure of bridges and other types of accidents could be deadly. The number of passengers who were killed in train wrecks in the year 1887, for example, was 207, with over 900 injured; as for railroad workers that year, there were 406 killed and 890 injured. Regardless of the dangers, the railroad became a powerful engine for the taming of the American West.

One such tragedy happened to the Pacific Railroad while it was pushing west across the state of Missouri. The headlines in the St. Louis *Daily Missouri Democrat* November 2, 1855, delivered the devastating, heartrending, breaking news to its waiting readers: "Terrible Catastrophe! The Excursion Cars to Jefferson City precipitated into the Gasconade River! Probable Death of many of our Distinguished Citizens!!"—and, on the very next day it simply read: "Latest News!! The Great Catastrophe." The inconceivable tale that unfolded shocked St. Louis, Missouri, and left many others in unbelief as to how such a disaster could have happened.

The Pacific Railroad was hard at work trying to complete track from St. Louis to Jefferson City, Missouri, and more was planned in its westward expansion. In order for the railroad company to continue its momentum, funds were needed. The state legislature

SHADES OF THE OLD, WILD WEST

was planning to convene sometime in November, and it was believed that a demonstration of progress might impress upon capital officials that the venture was a worthwhile project and, in the process, maybe obtain some much needed financial assistance from the state to continue on—so, an excursion train of about six hundred persons were going to make a first-run trip to Jefferson City from St. Louis. According to the St. Louis *Daily Missouri Democrat*, it read: "...leading merchants and railroad men of the city—judges of our courts and members of all professions—besides two companies of our military, the National Guards and the St. Louis Grays. Indeed, we may say, the very flower of our citizens were on board the train."

The decorated, 15-car party train left St. Louis at 9:00 a.m., November 1, 1855, on its maiden run to join the governor and other state officials on the grounds of the capital for a grand banquet hosted by the Pacific Railroad Company. As the excursion train passed Hermann, Mo., passengers aboard the steamboat, *Ben Bolt*, coming down the Missouri River preparing to land at Hermann, later reported that "the passengers both of the boat and cars exchanged greetings" as the train passed by them at 1:00 p.m., on its way to Jefferson City. It would be the last time that many souls aboard the train would ever be seen alive again.

About eight miles west of Hermann was the newly erected 900-foot trestle bridge over the mouth of the Gasconade River. The wooden structure was about thirty feet above the churning river and the ground below, and the waters of the Gasconade were about twenty feet deep. There was a final curve in the line just before the bridge, and according to the *Daily Missouri Democrat*, the "...bridge from all accounts was of the lightest material, and as stated by those who were on the spot, seemed little better than a work of scaffolding from which a heavier structure might have been reared. The strongest timbers were but six by nine scanting, upon which were laid strips of pine lumber, and to these were nailed the rails. Previously to the day of the excursion the bridge has been tried by the passing and repassing of the locomotive and construction train, but no test that we are aware of, equal in weight and magnitude to the excursion train, had ever been applied."

Pacific Railroad Disaster

The Gasconade Bridge, however, would not bear the weight of the 22-ton iron horse juggernaut and "the twelve cars of nearly ten tons each...driven at a speed of at least twelve miles per hour. The passengers were not generally apprised of the structure they were about to pass, and consequently had no fears as to its character for strength or security."

To make matters worse, "a tempest was pouring down its wrath" as the party train neared the bridge. From the train's tender, Hudson E. Bridge, the president of the Pacific Railroad, expressed his fears to chief engineer, Thomas S. O'Sullivan, "that the bridge might not be able to sustain the weight of the heavy train...." He proposed that the speed be reduced and that some of the passengers could disembark, "but the latter was sanguine of the strength of his work and gave no heed to the fears" of Bridge's foreboding premonition.

It was half past one o'clock in the afternoon when the train rounded the final curve in the track before the Gasconade Bridge. "There was no stopping of the train, but only a slackening of the speed, to make the passage more secure, and give persons on board an opportunity to viewing the structure.

"When the engine had just reached the edge of the second pier, the weight of the eight or ten of the heavily laden cars was too great, and the timbers gave way with a terrible crash." Below, was the muddy and rocky ground between the piers, and all but one hindmost car attached to a rear locomotive fell crashing down. The "shriek of the passengers as the bridge give way," was "represented as most terrible." About seventy souls per car found themselves instantly mingled in wreckage, as they "precipitated over an abutment, the one upon the other, each shivering to atoms as it fell, and scattering a thousand splinters and jagged fragments of iron and wood...."

All the while, storm clouds in the heavens above them continued their unforgiving work. The "merciless pouring of the rain and roar and flash of the angry tempest mingling with the cries of the wounded and dying, made a picture harrowing beyond anything the mind can imagine."

The locomotive that had been pushing at the rear of the train returned to Hermann with the startling news and to get help, then, returned to the bridge with some empty passenger cars to use as a makeshift ambulance in order to render further aid to the victims. Meanwhile, passengers at the scene who were able and willing began to offer assistance to their less fortunate companions of the party train that were injured or trapped in the mass of broken carriages; while others dealt with the sad and gruesome task of lifeless bodies.

Rescues were difficult under such circumstances, due to the raging storm, location, and condition of the wreckage. "The forward engine having just reached the second pier went down with the train, and as it fell turned completely over, and back upon the nearest cars, crushing the timbers and passengers in the most appalling manner. The middle cars were badly crushed by their own weight and those in the rear, precipitated with great violence over the abutment down upon the ruins beneath."

The carriages containing the St. Louis Grays and the National Guards were somehow thrown over on their sides, and were not crushed as others were. As a result, they faired better and were "saved from such dreadful injury."

As the news spread to St. Louis "general numbness" followed and the city was in mourning, as they waited with terror and anticipation for further updates in the grievous matter. They were shocked to learn that so many of their town's leading citizens were involved in such a terrible event. When the trains finally arrived conveying the dead and wounded to St. Louis—it lamented: "The quiet and peaceful hearts around many a fireside have been wrung with anguish by the great calamity that has recently befallen our city, while a veil of sadness has been cast over our entire community by the fatal summons that has hurried into eternity those who were most full of life and joy and promise amongst us. Nothing so sudden and so shocking has ever before befallen our people...when the news reached here that five hundred of those who had left the Pacific depots but a few hours previously, were hurled from the broken wreck of the Gasconade bridge, it caused a panic that we have never before witnessed. Throughout each day since the event and during the long interval of suspense before any definite news was had of casualties, almost all business was suspended—

Pacific Railroad Disaster

men were seen eagerly clustered together, inquiring for friends and relatives—and consternation pervaded every countenance. We hope earnestly it may never be our misfortune again to record such a dire event...."

It was noted that among the heroes at the recovery site were Ferdinand Kennett, George W. Alexander, Samuel Treat, Edwin Stephens, Isaac W. Green, John Hartnett and several others. However, also at the scene were some that were admonished for their behavior. "...we must reprobate in the strongest languages the conduct of those physicians who were wholly uninjured and who yet took the first occasion to desert the place of dire misfortune, where fractured limbs and agonized men were needing their help."

About thirty-four were killed in the disaster, which included: "Henry Chouteau, one of the oldest and most influential citizens; Rev. Dr. Bullard, of the First Presbyterian church; Capt. O'Flaherty; C.E. Blackburn, President of the Board of Aldermen; Mann Butler, Justice of the Peace; Thos. S. O'Sullivan, Chief Engineer of the Pacific Railroad; Thos. Gray; E.B. Dayton, Esq; Capt. [Calvin] Case; E.C. Yosti and Messrs. Mott, McCullough, of Dunkin, and Jeffries, Members of Legislature of this state. Messrs. Chappell, an old man, Lewis, Forsyth, Homes, Abeles, O'Neal, engineer, fireman and a German, names unknown, and a boy named Bill."

The good news was that, concerning the circumstances that out of such a large number of those involved in the accident, "precipitated as they were and crushed with the ruins of the broken cars, so few were killed." And, it was further added that: "Well indeed may we grieve when we recount the numbers of those that are lost, and, at the same time, well may we return thanks to a wonderful Providence that has preserved so many amidst the general ruin and disaster."

A special committee was formed to investigate the catastrophe. There were two theories that speculated that the curve in the line just before the bridge was a factor in the collapse. It was concluded, however, that had the train proceeded at a lower speed, the bridge may have been sufficient and the accident avoided, but the general impression seemed to be that the main source of the problem was the poorly constructed condition of the bridge.

SHADES OF THE OLD, WILD WEST

By the end of the American Civil War in April 1865, the legislature had, in spite of it all, funded the Missouri Pacific Railroad to link the states of Illinois and Kansas. On October 2, 1865, the first passenger train left Kansas City, Mo., and steamed across the newly rebuilt Gasconade Bridge—and, without further incident arrived to a relieved St. Louis about 18 hours later. The new steam powered technology was well on its way to carrying multitudes to the waiting West.

Bibliography

Book, Bill, *A Ticket to Tragedy*, Rural Missouri, Vol. 49, No. 9, September, 1996.

Clarke, Thomas Curtis, *The American Railway: Its Construction, Development, Management, and Trains*, Skyhorse Publishing, New York, N.Y., 2015.

Jackson, Rex T., *Notable Persons and Places in Missouri's History*, The Ozarks Reader, Neosho, Missouri, 2006.

Kreck, Dick, *Hell on Wheels: Wicked Towns along the Union Pacific Railroad*, Fulcrum Publishing, Golden, Colorado, 2013.

Parrish, William E.; Jones Jr., Charles T.; Christensen, Lawrence O., *The Heart of the Nation*, Forum Press, Inc., Arlington Heights, Illinois, 1980.

Other Sources:

St. Louis *Daily Missouri Democrat*, November 2, 3, & 5, 1855.

Steamboat A-Comin'

BEFORE the advent of the railroads, which quickly crossed and crisscrossed the nation, rivers were utilized as highways. Most of the times, to get from one place to another, rivers offered—at best, a winding and snake-like pathway to get there. The ride downstream was enhanced by the current, but traveling upstream against the flow was a different story altogether. This is where it took muscle, fortitude, ambition, know-how, ingenuity, and mechanical technologies. Over the years there were canoes, rafts, flatboats, keelboats, barges and other things to paddle, pole, push, pull, or float up and down America's plentiful waterways. With the coming of steam power, however, the sky was the limit. Before long, a new means of river-travel was conceived and unveiled—the steamboat, which blossomed to many different shapes and sizes in a short span of time.

One of America's first attempts at using a steam engine to propel a boat was by John Fitch, a clockmaker and silversmith who was born in 1743 on a farm in Connecticut. Fitch helped out during the American Revolution repairing guns for Revolutionary War soldiers—but, what he is best known for is his work with steamboats. In 1787, while the Constitutional Convention was in session, Fitch was experimenting on the Delaware River with a crude steamboat. The success of the first attempt led to another try in 1790, where his boat made a trip on the Delaware River carrying a number of excited passengers. He struggled with funds to continue

SHADES OF THE OLD, WILD WEST

Above: The *Clermont* (or *The North River*), from a photo taken of a replica in 1909. (From: *History of Our Country*, Reuben Post Halleck, American Book Company, 1923.)

Below: Henry Shreve's steamboat *Washington*. (From: *Fifty Years on the Mississippi: Gould's History of River Navigation*, Emerson W. Gould, Jones Printing Company, St. Louis, Missouri, 1889.)

his ambitions and eventually died in 1798.

Picking up where Fitch left off, though, was Robert Fulton, an artist from Lancaster, Pennsylvania who designed and built the first commercial steamboat, the *Clermont* (also known as *The North River*), which he demonstrated in 1807 by making a trip up the Hudson River from New York City to Albany, New York—about 150 miles, which took thirty-two hours to traverse. Fulton died eight years later.

The need for steam was building: there was lumber from the North Woods being floated downriver on simple rafts; and there were barges laden with their payloads of precious ore of lead and copper coming down from Wisconsin and Minnesota, and coal from the coal-rich states along the Ohio River in the East; and keelboats and flatboats hauling foodstuff, livestock, and supplies of all types using America's waterways. But the transportation of people was the most important cargo of all, and the age of steam power would herald in this nation-expanding era of river travel.

One man that did his share to further steamboat progress was Henry Miller Shreve, who was born in Burlington County, New Jersey, on October 21, 1785. When Henry was about three years old his family relocated to Fayette County, Pennsylvania, where he grew up along the banks of the Youghiogheny River and developed, much like Samuel Langhorne Clemens (Mark Twain), a lifelong fascination of river-ways and the boats that plied them.

By the time Shreve had reached the age of twenty-two he had built a keelboat at Brownville, Pa. on the Monogahela River, hired a crew and set off bound for St. Louis in October 1807. He bought a load of various goods at Pittsburgh and journeyed down the Ohio River toward the Mississippi River. It took forty days to reach St. Louis from Pittsburgh, and even longer to return there with his cargo of furs which he put on wagons bound for Philadelphia. It was the first direct fur trading route ever made between the two cities of Pennsylvania and Missouri.

Shreve continued in this way until 1816, when he built his own steam powered riverboat at Wheeling, West Virginia, called the *Washington*. It became the first two-deck steamboat on Western waters. Shreve placed the cabin between decks and the four single-flue boilers he placed, not in the hold but on deck. The high pressure engines of the *Washington* were put in a horizontal position. Shreve's new cam cut-off and boiler flues were able to save three-fifths of the steamboat's fuel.

The *Washington* left Wheeling on July 5, 1816, and arrived in New Orleans, Louisiana, by October 17. In Emerson W. Gould's book *Fifty Years on the Mississippi*, it reported that the "ascending voyage [the *Washington* made from New Orleans] was made in twenty-five days, and from this voyage all historians date the commencement of steam navigation in the Mississippi Valley." It proved that fire and steam could be used to ascend a river in one-fourth the time that it had taken a barge or keelboat, and so "her return trip to Louisville...demonstrated very clearly the possibility of ascending the river with steam. The trip of the Washington to Louisville was by far the most rapid made, up to that day."

Shreve's new showboat-style, two-deck *Washington* made it conceivable that grand, large scale riverboats could be built that could ascend the mightiest of all American rivers and comfortably carry passengers, crew and cargo to wharfs and landings all along the nation's waterways.

These grand steamers were a sight to behold, almost overnight Henry Shreve's two-deck style riverboat was adopted by many boat builders, and the idea blossomed to mightier proportions. Known as "showboats," these luxurious steamers boasted burlesque routines, gambling, acting troupes and musicians. One interesting sensation that was tried as a form of entertainment was the calliope (steam organ), which was first introduced on the Southern waters by the *Unicorn*, and on the Upper Mississippi by the *Excelsior*. When the public heard the new sounds echoing from the steam organ, many curious souls turned out to see what all the commotion was about. Expecting to see a large brass band or the like, they learned instead of the calliope. Its popularity on the boats that installed them left some passengers wishing, according to George Byron Merrick in his book *Old Times on the Upper Mississippi: The Recollections of a Steamboat Pilot from 1854 to 1863*, that "they had not come aboard, particularly if they were light sleepers. The river men did not mind it much, as they were used to noises of all kinds, and when they 'turned in' made a business of sleeping. It was different with most passengers, and a steam piano solo at three o'clock in the morning was a little too much for the money."

The most enduring entertainment tried on floating palaces during the steamboat era was the cabin orchestra, which turned out to be the cheapest to maintain and more widely accepted. Merrick wrote that: "A band of six or eight colored men who could play the violin, banjo, and guitar, and in addition sing well, was always a good investment...It soon became advertised abroad which boats carried the best orchestras, and such lost nothing in the way of patronage."

As for the bells and whistles that were used on the riverboats, they became recognizable sounds that helped to identify each one individually. Their steam whistles could be heard about five miles away, and as time went on they got bigger in size. Some could distinguish the whistle's pitch and resonance and knew which boat was coming. It was the same for riverboat bells, which ranged from five hundred pounds to fifteen hundred pounds. Reportedly, some of them were cast using a generous amount of melted silver dollars during their creation. The sounds that the bells produced were etched into the minds of their audiences, which left a romantic impression on some that never faded from their memories. This was the case of Merrick; one such bell that he became enchanted with prompted him to reminisce: "There was one, the music of which will live in my memory so long as life lasts. The tone of the 'Ocean Wave's' bell was deep, rich, sonorous, and when heard at a distance on a still, clear night, was concentrated sweetness. Were I rich, I would, were it possible, find that bell and hang it in some bell-less steeple where I might hear again its splendid tones, calling not alone to worship, but summoning for me from the misty past pictures indelibly printed upon boyish senses."

Most of the early boats burned wood for fuel. In the beginning the riverbanks were lined with lush timber, and many souls cashed-in and went to work providing firewood to passing steamers. As the demand continued to increase, large wood-yards sprang into existence a few miles apart along the rivers to cater to the demand. Before long, however, the hunger for wood to stoke the riverboat furnaces left the natural resources along the riverbanks, which some thought could never be depleted, stripped and clear-cut; a small boat could use about twenty-four cords of wood per day, while a larger packet could consume as much as seventy-five cords a day. Eventually, many steamboat packets converted to burning coal instead.

Steamboat travel also had its dangers and attracted its share of outlaws, pirates and highwaymen, like Mike Fink, Sam Gritty, the Murrel Gang, and the "Crow's Nest." The Murrel Gang, for example, who used the vast river system and canebrakes to elude capture, preyed upon their luckless victims. They would rob, steal slaves from "soul drivers," take horses, counterfeit, and commit murder. In a ghoulish confession offered up by the lawless Murrel after his capture, he testified, according to Emerson Gould, that: "They can never find that Negro, for his carcass has fed many a catfish and the frogs sung many a day to the silent repose of his skeleton." Such criminal activities became shameful stains upon the annals of American history.

As for the pirates that inhabited the Crow's Nest, which was located about 175 miles above Natchez, Mississippi, it was a base of operations in a thick forested area where there were caves and hidden coves to hide in; the outlaws would launch their thieving missions from this secluded haven upon their unlucky victims.

One of the most feared dangers awaiting passengers aboard a riverboat steamer was the threat of fire or an exploding boiler. One such disaster occurred on April 9, 1852, near Lexington, Missouri, on the Missouri River. In 1846, at Cincinnati, Ohio, a steamboat hull was built and delivered to St. Louis, Missouri, where it received two 30-foot boilers and two engines that were salvaged from a sunken wreck. The boat was dubbed the *Saluda*, which was 179 feet long, about 27 feet wide, and had two paddlewheels that measured 20 feet in diameter with buckets 10 feet long.

The *Saluda* had unfortunate luck from the beginning when it hit a snag near Rocheport, Mo., and sank. It was sold, raised, overhauled and back in business by 1848. Within three years it had new owners, and by 1852 Captain Francis T. Belt was half owner of the *Saluda*. Captain Belt was in his mid-30s and was considered to be a capable, experienced riverboat commander.

The task of maintaining a good safety record during the steamboat era was difficult because of river snags, sandbars, sawyers, ice packs, fires, boiler explosions and other dangers. The life expectancy of a river packet was reported to be about five years or less, and the *Saluda* was considered to be aging.

In early April 1852, the side-wheel steamer *Saluda* was en route from the major transfer point of St. Louis on the Missouri River headed west toward Kanesville (Council Bluffs), Iowa, and there was reported to be about two hundred or more persons aboard. The *Saluda* labored under power to overcome the ice floes and springtime currents at Lexington Bend, but without success. As a result, the steamer was forced to dock at Lexington's Upper Landing on April 4, 1852.

The greater part of the *Saluda's* passenger list were Mormons who had traveled from Europe in search of religious freedom. They were hoping to catch up with wagon trains of fellow believers-in-the-faith headed for Utah Territory. Other passengers were on their way to the West to try their luck in the goldfields of California. Also on board, besides the captain and crew, was valuable cargo—various goods, furniture and groceries.

The delay at Lexington because of the river conditions lingered for several days, and some passengers eventually disembarked in frustration. Finally, after the river was considered to be, for the most part, free of ice, on April 9, 1852, at 7:30 a.m., Captain Belt decided they had waited in Lexington long enough and ordered the crew to fire-up the boilers to maximum pressure. The *Saluda* had about 175 passengers left on board, as Captain Belt was reported to have said that he was going to "round the bend or blow this boat to hell."

Out of curiosity, many citizens of Lexington turned out for a chance to witness Captain Belt's brave attempt to defy the laws of nature—from their vantage ground along the wharf and atop the bluff where the town is perched. The *Saluda* let loose her mooring lines and eased out gently from Lexington Landing and into the stream, but no sooner had the boat's big paddlewheels made three determined revolutions when, all of a sudden the overburdened boilers blew simultaneously—the thunderous blast was heard for

Saluda Memorial at the Machpelah Cemetery in Lexington, Missouri.

miles! As a result of the explosion, two-thirds of the boat was torn asunder from the lower deck upward—all the way back to the wheel housings. What was left of the ill-fated *Saluda* started drifting back toward the levee as the stern began sinking below the waters of the Missouri.

Passengers and crewmen were blown in all directions, scalded, mangled, burned, limbs broken or torn off, or injured by flying debris. The victims who were able searched frantically for loved ones. Some were lost in the river's cold, spring currents while others were blown up on the riverbank.

The Lexington *Journal* reporting on the catastrophe a few days later on April 14, 1852, offered this gruesome account: "The mangled remains of human beings were scattered over the wharf and on the bluff; human blood, just warm from the heart, trickled down the banks and mingled with the water of the Missouri."

The boat's bell, which had so many times been heard on the river, was now laying boat-less high upon the bank. It was also reported that a 600 pound iron safe with a yellow-spotted dog leased to it, was cast through the air by the tremendous blast and landed on the bank—the dog was killed.

Citizens of Lexington came out in force to rescue or offer any assistance necessary to the poor victims of the disaster. Wounded sufferers were taken to makeshift hospitals—mostly at private residences along the upper end of the levee. And in time, they raised funds and found homes for the orphaned.

The number presumed to have perished as a result of probably the worst tragedy to occur on the Missouri River varied, from 26 to 135 dead or missing. Recorded on one of the *Saluda* Memorials in Lexington, estimates about 100 lost their lives. Captain Belt was killed and only three of his officers survived the ordeal.

Most of the victims were buried in a mass, common grave at the Machpelah Cemetery in Lexington; one of Missouri's celebrated graveyards established in 1849 by an act of the Missouri General Assembly. The cemetery is also the final resting place of early settlers, a mass grave of Confederate soldiers, prominent citizens, statesmen, explorers and others.

SHADES OF THE OLD, WILD WEST

The few who survived found other means of transportation and continued on their way. The loss of the *Saluda* caused the United States Congress that same year to institute new safety standards of operation for riverboat travel—but, it would come too late for the poor souls who lost their lives on the *Saluda* that cold, early spring morning.

On April 12, 2002, a new memorial was dedicated to the steamboat *Saluda* in downtown Lexington. It was created to honor and remember the lives of those who were tragically lost in the catastrophe.

The steamboat era hosted many unspeakable tragedies that suddenly visited many souls upon the rivers with scant warning and without mercy. On June 7, 1816, the *Washington*, under command of Captain Henry Miller Shreve, left Pittsburgh, Pa., on the Ohio River and arrived at Point Hamar the next day. On June 9, as the *Washington* was getting underway to continue down the Ohio, problems occurred with getting the machinery into proper starting condition. As a result, the river's current forced the boat toward the Virginia shore where it became necessary to deploy a kedge anchor to the rear of the boat. When crewmen were attempting to retrieve the anchor, however, the end of the cylinder in that part of the boat exploded, showering them in scalding, hot steam and water. According to James T. Lloyd's book *Lloyd's Steamboat Directory and Disasters on the Western Waters*, it inflicted "the most frightful injuries on nearly all the boat's crew, and killing a number on the spot. The cry of consternation and anguish which then arose might have been heard for miles."

Citizens and physicians of nearby Point Hamar quickly came to offer assistance and render whatever aid they could under the circumstances. The rescuers boarded the *Washington* to learn of the extent of the accident, "but no language can describe the scene of misery and torture which then presented itself to the view of the spectators. The deck was strewn with mangled and writhing human beings, uttering screams and groans of intense suffering. Some more fortunate than their companions, lay still in the embrace of death." Some tore off their clothes which retained their bodily skin, while others had their faces scalded beyond recognition. The worst, however, were those with internal injuries due to the inhalation of boiling steam. The catastrophe left victims "agonizing beyond all powers of imagination to conceive. The whole scene was too horrible for description, and it made an impression on the minds of those who witnessed it which could never be obliterated."

Many people were so frightened by the unforgettable event that they feared to continue steamboat travel. This was the first disaster of its kind on the Western waters—but, unfortunately, not the last.

When the *Louisiana* was preparing to leave New Orleans, Louisiana, for St. Louis, Missouri, on November 15, 1849, loaded mostly with a large number of Irish immigrants escaping from the potato famine which was plaguing the "Emerald Isle" (Ireland), an unthinkable thing occurred: "...all the boilers exploded with a concussion which shook all the houses for many squares around to their very foundations...The violence of the explosion was such, that large pieces of the boilers were blown hundreds of yards from the wharf, falling on the levee and in different parts of the city. One of these iron fragments cut a mule in two, and then struck a horse and dray, killing both driver and horse instantly...The sight of the mangled bodies on every side, the groans of the dying, and the shrieks of the agonized sufferers, produced a general thrill of horror among the crowd. The body of a man was seen, with the head and leg off, and entrails torn out. A woman, whose long hair lay wet and matted by her side, had one leg off, and her body was shockingly mangled. A large man having his skull mashed in, lay dead on the levee; his face looked as though it had been painted red, having been flayed by the scalding water. Other of both sexes, crushed, scalded, burned, mutilated and dismembered, lay about in every direction. Two bodies were found locked together, brought by death into a sudden and long embrace.

"But it is utterly impossible to describe all the revolting objects which presented themselves to the view of the beholders, suffice it to say, that death was there exhibited in all its most hideous forms; and yet the fate of many who still lived was more shocking and distressing than the ghastly and disfigured corpses of those whose sufferings were terminated by death."

Of the poor victims of the *Louisiana* who either died instantly or were later mercifully relieved of their struggles of life by the grim reaper, was believed to be between one hundred and fifty to two hundred lost souls.

But, by far the worst steamboat saga that ever occurred throughout America's dust bin of history happened to the ill-fated *Sultana* which exploded on the Mississippi River April 27, 1865, just north of Memphis, Tennessee. The boat's passengers were mostly jubilate Civil War veterans headed home after the war had just ended. These men had endured not just the death-hungry battlegrounds, but the unspeakable conditions and sufferings that existed at the infamous Andersonville and Cahaba Confederate prisons; they had just been recently released from their dreadful captivity. The *Sultana* was loaded at Vicksburg, Mississippi, totaling about 2,400 souls in all, which included the crew and other civilians—men, women, and children. When the boilers exploded on the overburdened boat laboring against the springtime current and snow melt, as many as 1,800 perished to fire and water—more than the famous, Irish-built *Titanic*.

One survivor of the *Sultana* recalled the horrendous scene: "Women and little children in their night clothes, brave men who have stood undaunted on many a battle field, all contribute to the confusion and horror of the scene as they suddenly see the impending death by fire, and wringing their hands, tossing their arms wildly in the air, with cries most heart-rending, they rush pell-mell over the guard into the dark, cold waters of the river."

The real tragedy concerning the *Sultana*, however, may have occurred afterwards when these Civil War veterans of long suffering and sacrifice were nearly forgotten by the nation and people they had served so bravely.

Regardless of the many tragedies, Henry Shreve's contribution to the steamboat era helped to bring in a new age and lifestyle for many Americans and immigrants searching for the excitement that could be found on the river. Shreve's boat and the many that followed in rapid secession which mirrored his original design, brought hoards to the West to settle in the fertile lands of the Mississippi Valley and beyond; and the many goods and supplies necessary to do so.

Steamboat A Comin'

Steamboats also contributed in many other ways, like the war efforts being waged all over the nation—both east and west of the Mississippi River fighting the bloody Civil War and for America's westward expansion, conquering Native Americans. Boats often transported troops and supplies in support of the military. One such riverboat steamer, which ended up becoming an American icon of the West, was the *Far West*; it was utilized and played an important part during and after the Battle of the Little Big Horn and the massacre of Custer and the Seventh Cavalry.

Built in 1870 in Pittsburg, Pennsylvania, the *Far West* was 190 feet long and 33 feet beam. It had two engines built by Herbertson Engine Works of Brownsville, Pa., which were fifteen-inches in diameter; and it was equipped with three boilers. The *Far West* was made for the Upper Mississippi trade, and had cabin spaces for about thirty passengers.

Under the command of Captain Grant Prince Marsh, the *Far West* was retained by the United States military to serve as a transport or patrol boat; it was also to be ready to act as a ferry, dispatch boat, gunboat, hospital boat, and as a headquarters, etc. On May 17, 1876, Lieutenant Colonel George Armstrong Custer and his Seventh Cavalry paraded around in Fort Abraham Lincoln with the regimental band playing one of their favorite tunes, *Garryowen*, an old Irish song; and as Custer and his army marched out of sight heading towards their doom at the Little Big Horn, in order to comfort their wives back at the fort, the band played *The Girl I Left Behind Me* as they faded into the distance.

By June 21, 1876, Captain Marsh and his steamer had made its way to the Little Big Horn River with supplies for the Seventh Cavalry. The *Far West* became a military headquarters that evening where war plans were hatched by Custer and two other generals. Early the next morning the supplies were unloaded and the army marched off. On June 25, 1876, while the *Far West* waited patiently at the mouth of the Little Big Horn overlooking the valley and the river beyond, Custer and his troops were making history.

News of what had befallen Custer and his army came by way of a Crow scout named Curley, who could not speak English but by pencil and paper and sign language delivered, to the best of his ability, the frantic story of their total annihilation. Aided by the river's current, Captain Marsh and his historic boat, about fifty-four hours after leaving the mouth of the Little Big Horn, carrying fifty-two wounded soldiers of General Reno's command, saw the twinkling lights of Bismarck looming ahead. No sooner had the *Far West* docked at the landing that men and officers scampered off through the streets spreading the news of the massacre to the slumbering Dakota town. Captain Marsh's trip down the Yellowstone River and the Missouri River to Bismarck was the fastest recorded time ever made by a steamboat.

The first published article concerning the massacre—about 2,500 words, was printed in the Bismarck *Tribune* dated July 6, 1876. It didn't take long for the revenge killing to commence. William F. Cody, better known as "Buffalo Bill," who was a chief scout for General George Crook, killed Cheyenne Chief Yellow Hand. After scalping him with his knife, Buffalo Bill waved the chief's scalp in the air, which still had his war-bonnet attached to it—and, in full view of the other oncoming braves, yelled out to them that it was only the first scalp to be taken in retaliation for the death of Custer at the Battle of the Little Big Horn (or the Battle of the Greasy Grass according to Native Americans).

Railroad tracks enabled passengers and cargo to travel a more direct route to destinations all over the country—and, as a result, steamboat travel in America waned. It was concerning this that Mark Twain may have said it best when he lamented: "Half a dozen sound-asleep steamboats…This is melancholy, this is woeful. The absence of the pervading and jocund steamboatman from the billiard-saloon was explained. His occupation is gone…Half a dozen lifeless steamboats, a mile of empty wharfs…Here was desolation indeed."

Bibliography

Dorsey, Florence L., *Master of the Mississippi: The Story of Henry Shreve, Who Taught a River to Fetch and Carry for the Nation*, The Riverside Press, Cambridge, Massachusetts, 1941.

Gould, Emerson W., *Fifty Years on the Mississippi: Gould's History of River Navigation*, Nixon-Jones Printing Company, 1889.

Halleck, Reuben Post, *History of Our Country*, American Book Company, 1923.

Hanson, Joseph Mills, *The Conquest of the Missouri: The Story of the Life and Exploits of Captain Grant Marsh*, A.C. McClurg, Chicago, Illinois, 1909.

Hartley, William G., and Woods, Fred E., *Explosion of the Steamboat Saluda: Tragedy and Compassion at Lexington, Missouri, 1852*, Missouri Historical Review, The State Historical Society of Missouri, 2005.

Havighurst, Walter, *Voices on the River: The Story of the Mississippi Waterways*, Castle Books, Edison, New Jersey, 2005.

Jackson, Rex T., *Notable Persons and Places in Missouri's History*, The Ozarks Reader, Neosho, Missouri, 2006; *The Sultana Saga: The Titanic of the Mississippi*, Heritage Books, Inc., Bowie, Maryland, 2003.

Lloyd, James T., *Lloyd's Steamboat Directory and Disasters on the Western Waters*, J.T. Lloyd and Company, Cincinnati, 1856.

Merrick, George Byron, *Old Times on the Upper Mississippi: The Recollections of a Steamboat Pilot from 1854 to 1863*, Arthur C. Clark Company, 1909.

Sandlin, Lee, *Wicked River: The Mississippi When it Last Ran Wild*, Vintage Books, New York, 2010.

Twain, Mark, *Life on the Mississippi*, American Publishing Company, Hartford, 1883.

Wright, Sara, *Steamboats: Icons of America's Rivers*, Shire Publications, Midland House, West Way, Botley, Oxford, U.K. 2013.

The Dalton Gang's Last Stand: Riding the Razor's Edge

FOLLOWING IN the footsteps of the James-Younger Gang who terrorized Missouri after the American Civil War, the Dalton Gang also chose to ride the razor's edge along the Owlhoot Trail. The life of these outlaws was somewhat intertwined, with ties to the "Outlaw State" and to each other—by flesh and blood and by rebel tendencies.

Lewis and Adeline Dalton, who lived in Cass County, Missouri (just south of Kansas City), had a big family of ten boys and five girls—most of them were born while they were living there. Lewis liked to drink alcoholic beverages and gamble on horse racing; while Adeline, when not giving birth, was a Christian Fundamentalist and had her hands full trying to raise their large brood. In order to make a living, Lewis owned a saloon—all in all, quite an environment on the home front. To top it off, however, Adeline was born a Younger; her brother was Henry Washington Younger, father of Cole, Jim, Bob, and John—who, for the most part, rode in the infamous James-Younger Gang; and they were also pro-Southern rebels who fought for, or favored the Confederacy during the Civil War. Henry was an influential man who was elected mayor of Harrisonville, Missouri in 1859; the town is located in the center of Cass County. On July 22, 1862, during the Civil War, Henry Younger was murdered—his body rifled. Just the kind of thing that helped to fuel the animosities that flourished in Missouri at the time.

SHADES OF THE OLD, WILD WEST

Above: Picture of Judge Isaac Parker in his courtroom in Fort Smith, Arkansas.
Below: Judge Isaac Parker's Court in Fort Smith, Arkansas.

Eventually, the Daltons packed out their trash and settled near Coffeyville, Kansas. Their oldest son, Frank, became one of Judge Isaac Parker's Deputy United States Marshals in 1884, policing the lawless Oklahoma Indian Territory. Judge Parker, however, gained his own fame and reputation as the "Hanging Judge" of Fort Smith, Arkansas. For twenty-one years starting on May 2, 1875, Judge Parker employed many U.S. marshals—red, white, and black to patrol the wild and wooly Indian Nations. His hangings became one of the Southwest frontier's most popular events, where crowds of death-loving spectators thronged to the main, neck-swinging attraction. Judge Parker's jail below the courtroom was known as the "Hell on the Border," and the gallows was dubbed "The Gates of Hell." Deputy U.S. Marshal Frank Dalton served Judge Parker with distinction until November 27, 1887, when Frank was killed in the line of duty serving a warrant on a man named Dave Smith who was wanted for horse theft and pedaling illegal whiskey. A heated gunfight ensued and Frank was hit in the chest; however, Frank had brought a helper to watch his back, Deputy U.S. Marshal James R. Cole who seized an opportunity and killed Smith. While all of this was taking place an outlaw who was with Smith, William Towerly, shoved his rifle into Frank's mouth and pulled the trigger; another heartless blast to the head finished the job.

After the death of Frank, brothers Grattan ("Grat"), Robert ("Bob"), and Emmett also tried their hand at being Deputy United States Marshals, but unhappy with the wages and dangers involved, and believing that they were being shortchanged, they abandoned their work as lawmen and converted to a life of crime. They traveled west to California and joined their brother William ("Bill"), and on February 6, 1891, they reportedly attempted to hold up the Southern Pacific Train No. 17 near the hamlet of Alila. The robbery didn't go as planned, a Wells, Fargo and Company employee, Charles Haswell, wielding a shotgun held them off. During their hasty retreat, though, fireman George Radcliffe was killed. As a result they fled to the safety of Oklahoma Indian Territory and on May 9, 1891, the Dalton Gang, accompanied by men like Bill Doolin, "Bitter Creek" Newcomb, Dick Broadwell, "Blackface" Charley Bryant, Bill Powers (alias Tim Evans), Charley Pierce, and William

SHADES OF THE OLD, WILD WEST

McElhanie, robbed the Santa Fe & Texas Express train at Wharton, Oklahoma. The Dalton Gang went on to hold up several other trains during this time period at Red Rock, Perry, the Cherokee Strip, and at Adair. However, not satisfied with the amount of loot they were splitting up between themselves robbing trains, and wanting to make a lazy get-a-way to South America, the Daltons decided to go out in style and knock off two banks at once—and in the process make history.

The lucky target became their hometown of Coffeyville, Kansas. The robbery attempt at Coffeyville was often compared to the botched nightmare which befell the James-Younger Gang in Northfield, Minnesota; located about forty miles south of the "Twin Cities" (St. Paul and Minneapolis). On September 7, 1876, Jesse and Frank James, along with Cole, Bob, and Jim Younger, and Charlie Pitts, Clell Miller, and Bill Chadwell, rode into the small, peaceful Scandinavian settlement hoping to make an easy score—presumably, a cakewalk. Towns like Northfield, Minnesota, however, would notice strangers like these from Missouri—to them, the Deep South. Their suspicions were spot on, though, and what followed quickly turned ugly. In twenty minutes the brigands were shot to pieces; the Youngers were captured but the James' escaped.

On October 5, 1892, sixteen years after the disaster at Northfield for the outlaws from Missouri, Bob, Grat, and Emmett Dalton, likewise, along with Bill Powers (Tim Evans) and Dick Broadwell rode into Kansas and down the streets of Coffeyville to their destiny with the C.M. Condon & Company Bank and the First National Bank. Wearing fake beards and mustaches in order not to be recognized in their hometown, the Daltons and their cohorts made their way along the dusty town thoroughfare past an observant man named Alex McKenna who was in front of a dry goods store. McKenna wasted no time spreading the news of the outlaws, as Bob and Emmett entered the First National Bank while Grat, Powers, and Broadwell disappeared into the C.M. Condon & Company Bank.

The citizen-army high-tailed it to the two stores in town that carried firearms and ammunition, Isham Brothers Hardware and Boswell Hardware; they were located on the east side of the town

The Dalton Gang's Last Stand

Illustration of the C.M. Condon & Company Bank in Coffeyville, Kansas.

plaza. When Bob and Emmett attempted to exit the First National Bank they were immediately showered with a hailstorm of lead. Quickly learning that it was a hopeless avenue, they darted back inside the bank and headed for a rear door instead. While making their way to the back of the bank they met Lucius Baldwin who was wielding a gun, and so Bob, taking no chances, shot him dead. Bob and Emmett left through the back entrance of the bank after having successfully confiscated a sack of about $20,000, and then headed for the alley where they had hitched their horses to a pipe.

Meanwhile, in the C.M. Condon & Company Bank, a tricky employee was able to convince Grat that the safe wouldn't open for another eight to ten minutes. So, as a result, the cashiers, Charles Ball and Charles Carpenter, were only forced to unload their cash drawers. After this, the outlaws charged out the door with their booty to face a barrage of gunfire, which left Grat, Powers, and Broadwell wounded as they raced for the alley to make their get-a-way.

The escape didn't go well; the alleyway became a turkey-shoot as the gun-battle intensified. When it was all said and done, four of the town's defenders, Lucius Baldwin, George Cubine, Charley Brown, and the City Marshal Charles T. Connelly, were killed as well as three others who were wounded. As for the Dalton Gang, only Emmett remained alive to tell the deadly tale—albeit, riddled with twenty-three bullet holes. The hitching-pipe alleyway where the majority of the firefight occurred became known as "Death Alley."

Soon after the shootout the riddled, lifeless bodies of the outlaw trophies were propped up and photographed—put on public display for people to gape at; hundreds were hauled-in on trains to catch a glimpse of the desperadoes—to get souvenirs or keepsakes of the historic event. Eventually, Bob and Grat Dalton, and Bill Powers were buried in the Coffeyville Cemetery; Bob and Grat had finally joined their older brother Frank who was already buried there after his murder in 1887 enforcing the law in Indian Territory. The locals, out of the goodness of their hearts, gave the robbers a piece of pipe for a grave marker—the same pipe that they had hitched their horses to in Death Alley; Emmett would, in later years, provide a more

The Dalton Gang's Last Stand

appropriate headstone.

Emmett Dalton faced his accusers and received a life sentence for his part in the crimes; he was sent to the Kansas State Penitentiary in Lansing, Kansas, just north of Kansas City, Kansas. Emmett was pardoned after only serving fourteen years of incarceration. He moved to Hollywood, California, sold real estate, married his childhood sweetheart and went on to write several books, some of which were made into movies. Besides acting in some films as well, he also, ironically, returned to Coffeyville and was a consultant on a movie filmed on location there about the Dalton's bank robberies. Emmett Dalton died on July 13, 1937, forty-five years after the Coffeyville raid.

The age of Wild West outlawry was beginning to wane, but before it faded away into America's dust bin of history, it would have to endure others, like Roy "Arkansas Tom" Daugherty and Henry Starr. Some contend that Starr's last robbery marked the end of the Old West outlaw era with his death and attempted heist and horseback get-a-way of a bank in Harrison, Arkansas, on February 18, 1921. Though crime continues to occur, lawlessness in the early days of America will forever be marked by the colorful, gun-totting individuals who chose to defy the government and the law—as they rode the razor's edge.

SHADES OF THE OLD, WILD WEST

Chronology

November 27, 1887—Deputy United States Marshal Frank Dalton is gunned down in Indian Territory while serving a warrant.

February 6, 1891—The Daltons attempt to rob a train in Alila, California.

May 9, 1891—The Dalton Gang holds up a train at Wharton, Oklahoma; other train robberies follow shortly after at: Red Rock, Perry, the Cherokee Strip, and Adair.

October 5, 1892—The Dalton Gang robs two banks in Coffeyville, Kansas, simultaneously; four of the town's defenders are killed and only Emmett Dalton survives the raid.

July 13, 1937—Emmett Dalton dies, forty-five years after the Coffeyville robberies.

Bibliography

Jackson, Rex T., *Traces of Ozarks Past: Outlaws, Icons, and Memorable Events*, Heritage Books, Inc., Berwyn Heights, Maryland, 2013.

Legrand, Jacque, *Chronicle of America*, Chronicle Publications, Inc., Mount Kisco, New York, 1989.

McNab, Chris, *Gunfighters: The Outlaws and Their Weapons*, Thunder Bay Press, San Diego, California, 2005.

Raine, William MacLeod, *Famous Sheriffs and Western Outlaws: Incredible True Stories of Wild West Showdowns and Frontier Justice*, Skyhorse Publishing, Inc., New York, N.Y., 2012.

Turner, George, *Gun Fighters*, L. Baxter Lane Publisher, Amarillo, Texas, 1972.

Wallis, Michael, *The Wild West 365*, Abrams, New York, N.Y., 2011.

Wexler, Bruce, *How the Wild West was Won: A Celebration of Cowboys, Gunfighters, Buffalo Soldiers, Sodbusters, Moonshiners, and the American Frontier*, Skyhorse Publishing, New York, N.Y., 2013.

Wood, Larry, *The Dalton Gang's Waterloo at Coffeyville*, The Ozarks Reader Extra, Vol. 2, Neosho, Missouri, 2005.

Minnesota the Beautiful and the Botched Mass Hanging

THE BATTLE for Minnesota lingered for hundreds of years: over its thousands of lakes and streams teeming with giant northern pike and walleye; its abundant, beautiful forests favored with plentiful wild edibles and game; as well as fertile farmlands for bountiful crops and produce; and other natural resources to entice the hearts of all who have found it or coveted it.

The first to inhabit present-day Minnesota and reap the benefits of its generosity were Native Americans, belonging to a branch of the Dakota Sioux. In the 1500s, the fortunate Sioux were being invaded by the Ojibwa (or Chippewa), which resulted in conflicts for about two hundred years over Minnesota's many gifts.

As war between the Sioux and the Ojibwa raged on, the first white men to venture into the region were a couple of French fur traders and explorers, Medard Chouard, Sieur des Grasseilliers and Pierre Esprit Radisson. Grasseilliers and Radisson made first contact with the Dakota Sioux somewhere along the Minnesota-Dakota border in 1660. Sioux delegates met with the Frenchmen that spring and invited them to visit the heartland of Minnesota. Grasseilliers and Radisson accepted and spent a month and a half with the Sioux.

On September 1, 1678, another French explorer, Daniel Greysolon Duluth (Dulhut or Du Lhut), set out on a secretive mission to the headwaters of the Mississippi River to try and make peace between the warring tribes in the region. A few months later the regional tribes assembled on the site of present-day Duluth,

SHADES OF THE OLD, WILD WEST

Indians attacking a white settlement.

(From: *History of Our Country*, Reuben Post Halleck, American Book Company, 1923.)

Minnesota the Beautiful

Minnesota—and, after the council, he headed to the Indian village of Nadouesioux near Milles Lacs Lake. Duluth eventually constructed a fortification along the banks of Lake Superior dubbed Fort Saint-Joseph on the site of present-day Detroit, Michigan, where he boldly proclaimed the entire region for France. However, by 1763 France's interest in Minnesota was ceded to the British until the Louisiana Purchase in 1803 when it became the property of the United States, despite the Sioux's indigenous first rights.

The early 1800s brought scores of white settlers into the embrace of Minnesota's natural wonders, which Native Americans had enjoyed for centuries—long before Europeans had set foot on the continent. In 1819, in order to protect the settlers, the first military base, Fort Saint Anthony was established; the fort was later renamed Fort Snelling. After treaties were signed with the Sioux (or the Santee Sioux) in 1851 giving up 28,000,000 acres to the United States, all they had left was a thin strip along the Minnesota River. By 1860, the "pale faces" had grown in number from about 5,000 to nearly 200,000 in population. Reduced to this, life for the Minnesota Sioux people became hard and they began to suffer when the government failed to send their promised annuities for all the land they had given up for money; and broken promises and unfair treatment from unscrupulous white traders, merchants, and U.S. Indian agents led to the "Minnesota outbreak" in 1862, which prompted violence against hundreds of white settlers in the region—and, many of them were killed. Chief Little Crow had cautioned against it, but in the end they chose the danger of retaliation.

Afterwards, there were battles fought against the U.S. government at places like New Ulm and Birch Coulee during the six-week Great Sioux Uprising on the Minnesota Frontier. The final clash in September 1862 at the Battle of Woods Lake left the Sioux deprived of their reservation—and, it also left more than 500 settlers and soldiers dead, as well as many Sioux. After the defeat of the Santee Sioux, which ended the Dakota War, the remainder of the tribe was herded to Camp Release where they awaited judgment. On September 28, 1862, Colonel Henry Hastings Sibley wrote to General John Pope to inform him that he was organizing a commission to try the Sioux warriors for their crimes, and if they

SHADES OF THE OLD, WILD WEST

were found to be guilty, executed.

In Washington D.C., President Abraham Lincoln took time out of his busy schedule of waging war—brother against brother, with the Confederate States of America—and all of his other duties, to review the problems in Minnesota and the fate of 392 Native American prisoners. It was clear what Minnesota Governor Alexander Ramsey wanted for the captive Sioux—either extermination or banishment. But President Lincoln made it clear that nothing was to be done to the prisoners without his approval. After six weeks of deliberation by the commission concerning the fate of the hated "red men," 303 were sentenced to death while the rest were to be incarcerated or acquitted.

When the time came to move the Sioux families, about fifteen hundred in all, to their winter location at Fort Snelling, they had to endure crowds of angry, hateful whites along the way shouting vile obscenities and attacking them—Indian men, women, and children with stones, clubs and other weapons. It was reported that one woman went so far as to snatch a nursing baby from the arms of a Sioux woman and, without remorse thrust the infant to the hard, frozen ground as hard as she could; they eventually made Fort Snelling on November 13, 1862. While the drum-fire of public, Christian vengeance increased for exterminating the "animals," President Lincoln gave his unpopular decision to stay the executions of 264 Sioux prisoners; however, one more was also saved from the hemp rope, which left thirty-eight condemned to hang.

The historic mass execution required a special place to carry it out. Mankato, Minnesota, was given the honors and a great, ingenious-made gallows was created and rose up between Front Street and the busy steamboat landing on the riverfront. The gallows was made in such a way that all of the condemned men could be hung simultaneously, as the platform in which they were standing on dropped down beneath them by the cutting of a single, central robe. On December 26, 1862, the morning after the celebration of the beloved Christian holiday—Christmas, thirty-eight Sioux braves judged and convicted of war crimes were led to the gallows where ropes were slipped over their heads; when all was ready, the command was given to the sounds of three drum-beats and the main

Minnesota the Beautiful

rope of the enginery of death was severed. While the platform fell away under their Sioux feet, cheers of joy ascended from the mouths of five thousand happy, white spectators. The ghastly entertainment continued for a full twenty minutes, as the poor souls daggled wildly and were tortured to death—choked and strangled because the execution was botched; the ropes were too long and, as a result, their necks were not snapped and they kicked and squirmed until death finally rescued them. So ended the largest mass execution conducted by the United States government in America's history.

Afterwards, their lifeless bodies were dropped into an unmarked hole—and, for the most part, forgotten. A few months later, the remainder of the Santee Sioux, over seventeen hundred in all, was marched out of Minnesota to waiting reservations in South Dakota and Nebraska. Like an elephant that never forgets, troops, apparently still seeking revenge for the Minnesota outbreak, attacked a Santee Sioux camp on September 3, 1863, at Maple Creek (Whitestone Hill), North Dakota—about 70 miles south of Jamestown. General Alfred Sully and about 2,000 troops massacred about 200 Indian men, women, and children as they scampered away from their Indian village. General Sully obliterated what was left of the Indian camp and took home his trophy of about 156 Sioux prisoners.

In the end, Native Americans who had bask in the beauty, plenty, and firesides of Minnesota for centuries, free to pursue life according to their own chosen lifestyle, could only reminisce and seethe and boil and stew over such an important loss to their people.

SHADES OF THE OLD, WILD WEST

Chronology

1500s—The Sioux in Minnesota were being encroached upon by the Ojibwa Indians which resulted in conflicts.

1660—Medard Chouart, Sieur des Grasseilliers and Pierre Esprit Radisson, two French fur traders and explorers, made first contact with the Dakota Sioux.

September 1, 1678—Daniel Greysolon Duluth, another French explorer, set out on a secret mission to try and make peace with the warring tribes.

1803—The Louisiana Purchase.

1819—The first military base, Fort Snelling, is established.

1851—Santee Sioux give up 28,000,000 acres to the United States.

1862—Great Sioux Uprising.

September 1862—Battle of Woods Lake and the end of the Minnesota outbreak.

November 13, 1862—Thirty-eight Santee Sioux prisoners are hung at a botched public execution in Mankato, Minnesota.

September 3, 1863—U.S. troops under General Alfred Sully attack Santee Sioux Indians at Whitestone Hill, North Dakota, and kill about 200 Indian men, women, and children and take 156 prisoners.

Bibliography

Berg, Scott W., *38 Nooses: Lincoln, Little Crow, and the Beginning of the Frontier's End*, Pantheon Books, New York, 2012.

Funk & Wagnalls New Encyclopedia, Funk & Wagnalls, Inc., New York, 1979.

Golay, Michael, and Bowman, John S., *North American Exploration*, Castle Books, Edison, New Jersey, 2006.

Legrand, Jacques, *Chronicle of America*, Chronicle Publications, Inc., Mount Kisco, New York, 1989.

Wallis, Michael, *The Wild West 365*, Abrams, New York, N.Y., 2011.

Goodnight-Loving Trail: The Life and Times of Goodnight, Loving, and Adair

REMINISCENT of the old Western television shows and movies, the herding of cattle across long distances was undertaken by daring, rough and rugged cowpokes. These ranchers and Old West trail-drivers rode in the saddle for hours and ate all the trail dust that came their way. They slept under the nighttime stars and feasted on the grub that the "chuck wagon" cooks prepared for them while they entertained themselves with cowboy bravado around the campfire. Though the American West boasts of many of these hardened characters, names like Charles Goodnight, Oliver Loving, and John Adair often rise to the surface to bask in the era's spotlight.

Charles Goodnight was born in Macoupin County, Illinois, located just northeast of St. Louis, Missouri, in March 1836. When he was about ten years old he moved to Texas and before long had joined the Texas Rangers where he helped to keep the peace between settlers and the Comanche Indians. When the American Civil War erupted, Goodnight served in the Confederate army. In 1866, the next year after the War Between the States had ended, Goodnight met Oliver Loving; the two had a lot in common and decided to team up on a money-making venture to drive a herd of feral (wild) Longhorns from Young County, which was located near Graham, Texas, to Fort Sumner, New Mexico Territory. The idea was to supply beef to thousands of Navajo Indians who had been

SHADES OF THE OLD, WILD WEST

Above: Illustration of Western saddles. (From: *When a Man's a Man*, Harold Bell Wright, A.L. Burt Company, New York, 1916.) Below: Illustration of a cowboy lassoing a steer. (From: *History of Our Country*, American Book Company, New York, 1923.)

relocated to the fort and were in desperate need. From there, they planned to head north to Denver, Colorado. After their delivery was made to Fort Sumner, Goodnight headed back to Texas to begin rounding up another herd while Loving drove what was left of the herd to Denver and sold them to a man named John W. Iliff. The route which the two partners blazed became known as the Goodnight-Loving Trail.

While Oliver Loving was on his way back to rejoin Goodnight in Texas, he was ambushed by a Comanche war party and was severely injured. Loving eventually died at Fort Sumner; after Goodnight had driven his new herd down the Goodnight-Loving Trail to Colorado, he stopped at Fort Sumner on his way back through and retrieved his partner's remains in order to take him back to Texas for a proper burial. Before long, the historic trail from Texas to Colorado was extended to include Wyoming—a long way to drive cattle. By 1869 Goodnight had his own ranch in Colorado on the Arkansas River and had married Mary Anne Dyer. While there, he helped to establish the Stock Growers Bank in Pueblo, Colorado; but the Panic of 1873, which began on September 20 after the New York City Stock Exchange closed in panic, following a rash of ruined firms starting with the Jay Cooke & Company—a supporter of the Northern Pacific Railroad. The panic was blamed on not enough currency and too much speculation. Three years later Goodnight and Mary packed up and headed for Texas.

Goodnight once again took on a partner in 1876, an Irish immigrant, financier John Adair, and settled on a massive 1,335,000 acre ranch in the southern part of the Texas Panhandle at Palo Duro Canyon; Goodnight would go on to be dubbed the "father of the Texas Panhandle."

As for John George Adair, who was born in Ireland in 1823, a descendant of Scottish-Irish Protestants, he attended the famous Trinity College in Dublin, Ireland, and studied business. He came from a well-to-do landholding family line. As a result, Adair built an impressive granite manor in 1870 on the shores of Lough Beagh in County Donegal (the most northwestern county in Ireland), called Glenveagh Castle. His popularity in the "Emerald Isle" waned, however, after he evicted some poor tenants with small-holdings during Ireland's Great Famine. The famine in County Donegal went on to prompt vigorous immigration as a result of social disruption, economic decline, hard times, and the mortality rate. Adair joined the crowd and migrated to America himself to take advantage of the opportunities in the West. When Adair was brought home to Killenard, Ireland, after his death, it was reported that locals tossed a dead dog into his grave as a sign of their disapproval of his earlier actions—evicting families to landscape the surrounding grounds of Glenveagh Castle.

Goodnight's ranch at Palo Duro Canyon was named J.A. Ranch after the Irishman, Adair. Besides Goodnight's work breeding cattle and crossbreeding cattle with buffalo, which he called "cattalo," his herd of American bison helped to save the iconic species from extinction. Mary Anne Goodnight passed away in 1926, and Charles Goodnight lingered another few years and bit the dust in 1929.

Bibliography

Anderson, Janice, *A Celebration of Ireland*, Hermes House, London, U.K., 2010.

Lalor, Brian, *The Encyclopedia of Ireland*, Yale University Press, New Haven and London, 2003.

Legrand, Jacques, *Chronicle of America*, Chronicle Publications, Inc., Mount Kisco, New York, 1989.

Turner, Erin H., *It Happened in the Old West*, Twodot, Guilford, Connecticut, 2017.

Wallis, Michael, *The Wild West 365*, Abrams, New York, N.Y., 2011.

Wexler, Bruce, *How the Wild West was Won: A Celebration of Cowboys, Gunfighters, Buffalo Soldiers, Sodbusters, Moonshiners, and the American Frontier*, Skyhorse Publishing, New York, N.Y., 2013.

John Wesley Hardin: A Homicidal Desperado

THE LAWLESSNESS that existed in Western cow towns, railroad towns, and mining towns was sometimes the result of criminal-minded individuals migrating there to take advantage of such innocent, vulnerable places. And not all outlaws came from the usual suspected lifestyles. Such is the case of John Wesley Hardin who became one of the Old West's most infamous and prolific homicidal killers.

John Wesley Hardin was born in Bonham, Texas, on May 26, 1853, to James G. Hardin and Mary Elizabeth Dixon Hardin. John's father, who was a Methodist minister and school teacher, endeavored to raise his son in a punctilious Christian environment—making him study the Holy Bible, attend church, and conduct his outward appearance with religious piousness. In order to complete his perfect offspring, James Hardin blessed his son with the name of the founder of his Methodist religion, John Wesley.

The worldwide Protestant movement of Methodism began in 1729 when a group of students attending the University of Oxford, England, began to congregate privately for Christian services. They were eventually dubbed "Oxford's Holy Club" and "Methodists" by their fellow students at the university; John Wesley was part of the group and considered to be the founder of the Methodist religion. The Wesleyan Revival sought to make improvements on the Church of England by paying strict and rigid attention to the sacraments. In order to create this doctrine of Christian perfection, John Wesley

SHADES OF THE OLD, WILD WEST

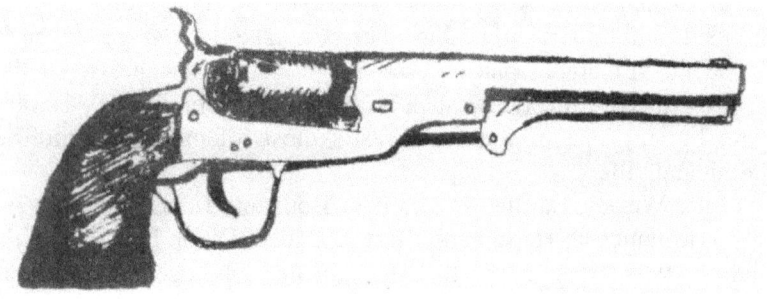

Illustration of a Colt revolver.

John Wesley Hardin

preached and his brother Charles Wesley wrote hymns. In February 1737, Reverend John Wesley arrived in America to take over the title of chaplain at the Georgia colony—the Methodist founder had come to America.

After John Wesley Hardin had received his father's dedicated Christian instructions and Methodist upbringing, at the tender age of fifteen he killed his first man. In November 1868, three years after the end of the American Civil War which left Confederate Texas with African American freedmen, Hardin, while visiting his uncle's plantation near Moscow, Texas, shot and killed an ex-slave named Mage (or Maje). As a result, three Texas Rangers were dispatched to apprehend Hardin for murder but he turned the table on them and ambushed the lawmen, killing two with a shotgun and the other one with his pistol. Some explanations for his first murder included the fact that he was known to be an advocate and follower of the white supremacist group the Ku Klux Klan.

The "Klan" was an anti-black organization formed in Pulaski, Tennessee, in December 1865—a few months after the end of the Civil War. The secret society was known to dawn white hooded robes and ride under the cover of darkness for their missions of discrimination and hate. The leader of the Ku Klux Klan was the ex-Confederate General Nathan Bedford Forrest, known as the "Grand Wizard." The organization attracted the deplorable element—racists, anarchists, ex-rebels, anti-government, etc., and was quickly welcomed from Tennessee to Texas and all across the Deep South and other places.

Hardin practiced his deadly craft daily, and carried concealed guns in holsters sewn into his garments across his chest. He reportedly ended the lives of more ex-slaves as well as a card shark named Jim Bradley in 1869; a Waco, Texas, Marshal L.J. Hoffman; and Jim Smally, another Texas lawman. In 1871, trying to stay ahead of the law, he signed on as a cowboy and headed towards Abilene, Kansas, over the Chisholm Trail.

The first Texas Longhorns driven along the Chisholm Trail to the Abilene railhead happened on September 5, 1867, when 35,000 Longhorns arrived there on their way to markets back East. The event was dubbed "the long drive" which started in South Texas and ended in the small "hell on wheels" railroad town of Abilene, Kansas. En route, Hardin reportedly added a few more notches to his gun before reaching Abilene in June 1871. While in Abilene, he met and befriended—to some degree, "Wild Bill" Hickok and Ben Thompson; Hickok was the town constable and Thompson owned the Bull's Head Saloon. When he arrived in Abilene, Hardin checked-in to the American House Hotel where he supposedly committed one of his most senseless, legendary crimes—he shot and killed a man for snoring in the adjacent room, firing two shots through the wall because he couldn't sleep. Instead of facing Hickok, Hardin jumped from his second story window to the street below and hightailed-it out of Abilene and back to the sanctuary of Texas; he never returned to Abilene, Kansas.

Back in Texas he settled down in Comanche, located about seventy-five miles southeast of Abilene, Texas, and in May 1874, just before he turned twenty-one, he had a shoot-out with Deputy Sheriff Charles Webb. Hardin was wounded in the exchange, but Webb, shot in the face did not survive. After he escaped, a mob formed and avenged the death of Webb by lynching his brother Joe Hardin and his cousins, Tom and Bud Dixon.

After wandering about throughout the South he landed in Pensacola, Florida, where he was eventually arrested at Pensacola Junction and taken into custody by Texas Rangers in early August 1877. He was sentenced to only twenty-five years in the Texas State Penitentiary in Huntsville for murder. Hardin, now twenty-four years old, was said to have killed at least forty men. Ironically, though, while incarcerated at Huntsville he flattered his namesake by studying Wesleyan theology and law.

On February 17, 1894, after serving seventeen years of his sentence, Texas Governor Jim Hogg awarded Hardin his freedom. He moved near El Paso, Texas, and after passing the bar exams, opened up a law practice—of all things, in Gonzales, Texas.

Finally, on August 19, 1895, John Wesley Hardin was killed at the Acme Saloon in El Paso. The "dark angel of Texas" was having a drink and doing a bit of gambling with bartender Henry Brown when Sheriff John Selman, who feared for his son's life after he was threatened by Hardin, moseyed up to the legendary killer and plugged him three times—the fatal, magic bullet was said to have put a large hole in the back of his hat.

The death of the infamous gunslinger, outlaw, murderer, and Wesleyan brought an end to at least one "wolf in sheep's clothing"—but, the religious-rooted man that once said that he would "take no sass but sasparilla," was true to his word until the moment of his own violent demise.

SHADES OF THE OLD, WILD WEST

Chronology

1729—Methodist religion was born.

February 1737—Reverend John Wesley arrives in America and becomes chaplain in the Georgia colony.

May 26, 1853—John Wesley Hardin was born in Bonham, Texas, to James G. Hardin and Mary Elizabeth Dixon Hardin.

December 1865—The Ku Klux Klan is established.

September 5, 1867—35,000 Longhorn cattle arrive in Abilene, Kansas, over the Chisholm Trail.

November 1868—John Wesley Hardin kills his first man.

June 1871—Hardin reaches Abilene, Kansas, and checks-in to the American House Hotel.

May 1874—Back in Texas Hardin kills Deputy Sheriff Charles Webb.

August 1877—Hardin is arrested in Pensacola, Florida, and sentenced to twenty-five years in the Texas State Penitentiary.

August 19, 1895—John Wesley Hardin is gunned down in El Paso, Texas, by Sheriff John Selman. It was believed that Hardin had killed at least forty men in his lifetime.

John Wesley Hardin

Bibliography

Cimino, Al, *Gunfighters: A Chronicle of Dangerous Men and Violent Death*, Chartwell, New York, N.Y., 2016.

Funk & Wagnalls New Encyclopedia, Funk & Wagnalls, Inc., New York, 1979.

Legrand, Jacques, *Chronicle of America*, Chronicle Publications, Inc., Mount Kisco, New York, 1989.

McNab, Chris, *Gunfighters: The Outlaws and Their Weapons*, Thunder Bay Press, San Diego, California, 2005.

Turner, George, *Gun Fighters*, L. Baxter Lane Publisher, Amarillo, Texas, 1972.

Wallis, Michael, *The Wild West 365*, Abrams, New York, N.Y., 2011.

Wexler, Bruce, *How the West was Won: The Gunfighters*, Skyhorse Publishing, New York, N.Y., 2016.

Henry Starr:
Robber with Distinction

THE WILD WEST endured its share of bank and train robberies during the nineteenth century, and some of them spilled over into the twentieth century. One such bank robbery which occurred in 1921 had the distinction of being the first time that the crooks showed up in an automobile; some argue that this bank heist also marked the end of the Old West outlaw era, after the gang was forced to burn and abandon their automobile and make their get-a-way on stolen horses. The end of the gun-totting, horseback riding outlaw, like you see in the movies, would at long last fade into American history—it would end with Henry Starr.

Henry Starr was born on December 2, 1873, near Fort Gibson in Indian Territory. Henry was born to George "Hop" and Mary Scot Starr who were part Cherokee. His grandfather was Tom Starr, an outlaw, and his uncle was the notorious Sam Starr who was Belle Starr's second husband.

When Starr was only thirteen years old his father died and his mother remarried C.N. Walker—they didn't "get-along". Henry left home a few years later in 1889 and so began his run-ins with the law. While living in the Nowata area of Indian Territory he was caught with illegal whiskey. A couple of years later in 1891 he was arrested for horse theft and incarcerated in Ft. Smith, Arkansas; after jumping bail he became a wanted man. At this time, Starr teamed up with some other unsavory characters and his gang robbed the Nowata Train Depot in July 1892. A few months later in November

153

HENRY STARR, THE NOTORIOUS OUTLAW IS SHOT HERE.

W. J. Myers, formerly of the Peoples Bank, Shoots Starr from Bank Vault While Attempting Robbery.

Headlines from the Harrison *Times*, February 19, 1921.

they hit the Shufelds Store in Lenapah and the Carter Store in Sequoyah—both in the Nations. In 1908, Starr and his gang knocked off a bank at Tyro, Kansas, and then hightailed it back to Oklahoma. In 1913, after an arrest and conviction, Starr was paroled from the Canon City Penitentiary in Colorado. He's back in business by 1914 after robbing the Farmers State Bank in Glencoe, Oklahoma; it becomes one of several daytime bank heists launched by the outlaw from September 8, 1914, to January 13, 1915.

Starr's lawless adventures came to a halt on March 27, 1915, while attempting to knock off two banks at once—a feat the Dalton Gang failed to do in Coffeyville, Kansas in 1892. Henry Starr and six cohorts rode into Stroud, Oklahoma and proceeded to hold up, simultaneously, the Stroud National Bank and the First National Bank. As a result, Starr and another gang member were wounded in a firefight with citizens and taken into custody; the other robbers made history and made off with the loot. Because of this, Starr went on to spend time in the Oklahoma State Penitentiary. While imprisoned at the facility located in McAlester, he had a change of heart and vowed to go straight. He was paroled on March 15, 1919, for his good behavior.

Henry Starr's law abiding about-face lasted a couple of years when he became involved in Hollywood filmmaking, producing and starring in a silent movie depicting the Shroud bank robbery called *A Debtor to the Law*; as well as a few other silent movie films. It was during this hiatus from crime that he met and wed his wife, Hulda, of Salisaw, Oklahoma, on February 22, 1920, and moved to Claremore. However, the life of an outlaw was in his blood and Henry Starr's law-abiding streak came to finality about a year later.

Starr and three of his cronies stole a car—a Nash, in Claremore belonging to a man named Rogers and headed for Harrison, Arkansas; however, it was reported that Starr robbed a bank in Seligman, Missouri, in December 1920, just before Christmas. When the Starr Gang made Harrison, though, on February 18, 1921, they parked their Nash and strolled into the Peoples National Bank of that Boone County town and according to the Harrison *Times*: "The first attempt at bank robbery in the history of Harrison [another distinction], was staged this morning shortly after ten

SHADES OF THE OLD, WILD WEST

o'clock at the Peoples National Bank, when Henry Starr, the notorious Oklahoma outlaw [sometimes referred to as "The Bearcat"], of national ill repute, and three confederates entered the bank with drawn guns and ordered 'hands up.'"

Starr's men had the drop on the bank's cashier, Cleve Coffman, and according to the *Times*: "The affair was conducted by a master hand at this outlaw game...." The bank president Marvin Wagley and Cleve Coffman, facing the bandit's .45 caliber pistols, were left with the option of obeying their desperate orders. However, also in the bank, ironically, was a former employee, William J. Myers who knew where a rifle—a Winchester Model 1873 was hidden in the back of the vault. Myers, seizing an opportunity, with "coolness and courage...stepped into the vault, secured [the] rifle and fired on Starr while he was looting the open safe of its contents."

Dazed but not confused from the blast of Myers' Winchester and "feeling himself mortally wounded, at once saw the game was up, and ordered his confederates who were making as if to shoot Cashier Cleve Coffman, to leave without shooting anyone...." Starr may have saved Cashier Coffman's life in doing so.

When Starr's gang realized the gig was up, they fled the scene and headed for their get-a-way car which had been left on the west side of the bank. The *Times* reported that they "departed over the Crooked Creek Bridge, exchanging fire with Mr. Myers, who rushed out of the bank and fired on them as they departed." Myers managed to blow out their windshield and hit one of the tires on the car.

A number of armed men immediately organized a posse to pursue the armed bandits, but returned saying that they could only "see them fleeing in the distance." It was reported that the robbers burned their vehicle near Bellefonte (an old community in Boone County that grew up near a spring prior to the American Civil War) and disappeared into the surrounding woodlands cutting "telephone wires as they went." They eventually stole some horses to further their get-a-way—making it the last horseback robbery in American history.

Meanwhile, Henry Starr was taken to the Harrison jailhouse where physicians attended to his mortal wound. "The ball had penetrated into a vital part [of his spine] inflicting partial paralysis, and an incision was necessary to remove it," said the *Times*. Starr asked for chloroform and while he was undergoing treatment he requested to see Cashier Coffman to beg for his forgiveness and to find out who had shot him. When Coffman arrived Starr shook his hand and said: "You know I saved your life." The dying outlaw also wanted Coffman to remain at his side and wished for him to have his gun and that his family be "notified of his mishap." About W.J. Myers, he said: "I do not blame him at all, I would have done the same thing in his place. He was at one end of the game, and I at the other, and he won. He has a cool hand." On his lingering deathbed Starr went on to claim that he had "robbed more banks than any other man in the United States." He also stated that "he had never killed a man in the course of his career as an outlaw, and was glad that he had not."

Henry Starr, one of the nation's last Old West outlaws, died at the county jail on a cot February 22, 1921; four days after the attempted robbery. Because of his lingering condition some of his family was able to be present when he expired. His remains were accompanied back to Oklahoma by his "mother, Mrs. Mary Gordon, wife Mrs. Henry Starr, son Theodore Roosevelt Starr of Muskogee [Okla.], son Tonnie Starr of Homer, La., nephew Emmet Daughtery and sister Mrs. Ewing and husband." He was taken to Dewey Cemetery in Dewey, Oklahoma, and buried next to "his sister and his child [Baby Starr]"—his gravesite has no marker.

About Henry, his mother was quoted as saying about the day of his birth that: "Henry has always been a trial to me." "But, thank God," she went on to say, "I will know where he is tonight. I believe his character was being molded even before his birth. There was a serious uprising in Oklahoma in those days, and those dark, dangerous days must have had a prenatal influence."

The last words the dying bandit was able to speak to his mother was: "Mother, I am satisfied to die—I have made my peace with God." His final advice to his son was that he should "go straight," and "expressed regret to him for the stain placed on his name."

The bank offered a five hundred dollar reward for the arrest and conviction of the rest of the gang. The search for Starr's accomplices-in-the-crime was ongoing after he divulged their names to the authorities before he died.

Another similar outlaw of the Wild West, Roy "Arkansas Tom" Daugherty, who was eventually shot and killed in Joplin, Missouri, on August 16, 1924, ended his career using automobiles on a number of occasions. Henry Starr's work in Harrison makes him a prime historical candidate-suspect of the possible distinction of heralding in the end of the Old West outlaw era.

Bibliography

Cimino, Al, *Gunfighters: A Chronicle of Dangerous Men and Violent Death*, Chartwell Books, New York, N.Y., 2016.

Jackson, Rex T., *Traces of Ozarks Past: Outlaws, Icons, and Memorable Events*, Heritage Books, Inc., Berwyn Heights, Maryland, 2013.

McNab, Chris, *Gunfighters: The Outlaws and Their Weapons*, Thunder Bay Press, San Diego, California, 2005.

Wallis, Michael, *The Wild West 365*, Abrams, New York, N.Y., 2011.

Young, Richard Alan, and Judy Dockrey, *Outlaw Tales: Legends, Myths, and Folklore from America's Middle Border*, August House, Little Rock, Arkansas, 1992.

Other Sources:

Harrison *Times*, February 19, 22, 26, 1921.

Additional Illustrations

A steam engine, tender, and passenger car.

An early nineteenth century locomotive and train.

(From: *History of Our Country*, Reuben Post Halleck, American Book Company, New York, 1923.)

Above: Fort Smith National Historic Site, Fort Smith, Arkansas.
Below: Judge Isaac Parker's Courtroom at Fort Smith, Arkansas.

Above: Nineteenth century steamboat.
(From: *Little Journeys to Alaska and Canada*,
Marian M. George, A. Flanagan Company, Chicago, 1901.)

Below: Illustration of a covered wagon headed west.
(From: *History of Our Country*, Reuben Post Halleck,
American Book Company, New York, 1923.)

Indian teepee and family.

(From: *Little Journeys to Alaska and Canada*,
Marion M. George, A. Flanagan Company, Chicago, 1901.)

An Indian boy.

(From: *Little Journeys to Alaska and Canada*,
Marion M. George, A. Flanagan Company, Chicago, 1901.)

Native American camp.

(From: *Little Journeys to Alaska and Canada*,
Marion M. George, A. Flanagan Company, Chicago, 1901.)

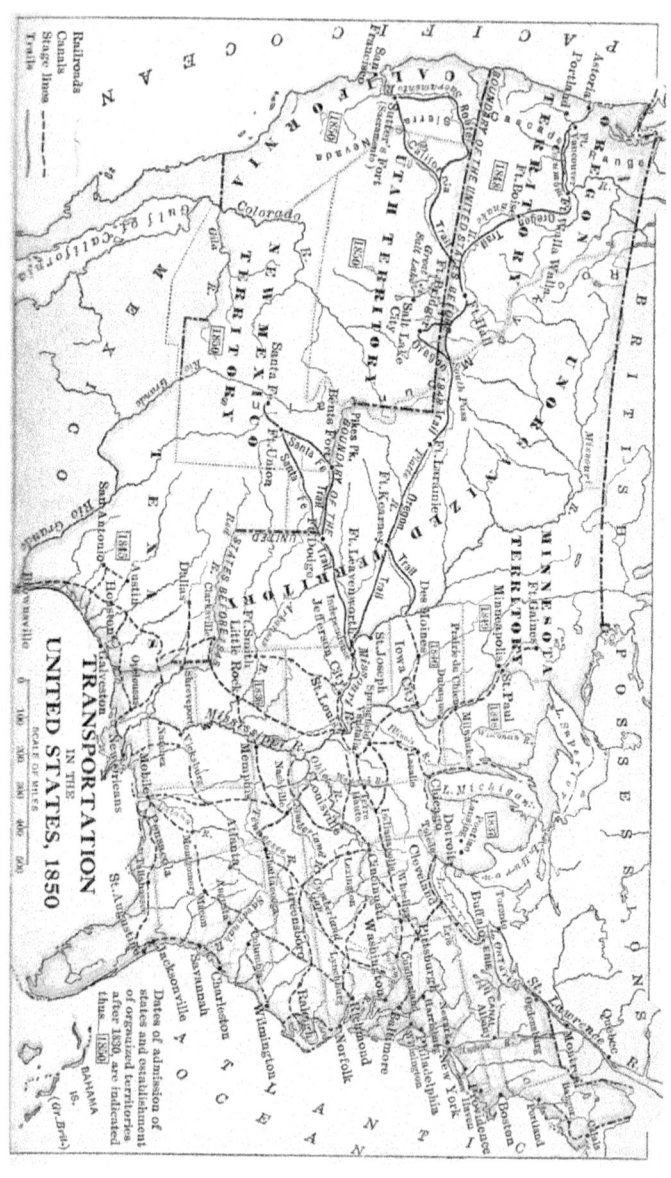

Transportation in the United States in 1850.

(From: *History of Our Country*, Reuben Post Halleck, American Book Company, New York, 1923.)

The American Bison; it was reported that by 1889 less than 600 of them remained.

Index

Index

A

Abilene, Kansas, 147, 148
Abilene, Texas, 148
Adair, John George, 139, 141, 142
Alexander, George W., 101
Anna, Santa, 5
Ault, A.F., 23
Austin, Moses, 11
Austin, Stephen Fuller, 11

B

Baldwin, Lucius, 126
Bassett, Charley, 19
Behan, John, 69
Belfast, Ireland, 2
Bell, J.W., x
Belt, Francis T., 110, 111
Bender, Kate, 51, 53, 54, 56
Bent's Fort, 3
Bigler, John, 11
Billy the Kid, ix, x
Bismarck *Tribune*, 118

Black Kettle, Chief, 79, 80, 81, 83, 84, 85, 86
Bolivia, San Vicente, xi
Bonney, William Henry, ix
Boudinot, Elias, 89
Bowie, James, 5
Brannan, Samuel, 9
Broadwell, Dick, 20, 123, 124
Brown, Charley, 126
Butler, Frank, xii
Butterfield Overland Mail, 2

C

Cannary, Martha Jane, 59, 60, 61, 62, 63, 64
California *Star*, 9
Carson, Christopher, 90, 92
Carthage, Missouri, 41, 43
Cassidy, Butch, xi
Chicago, Illinois, 31, 35
Chivington, John Milton, 80, 81
Chouteau, Henry, 101
Claiborne, William C., 74
Clanton, Billy, 74
Clanton, Ike, 73, 74
Clark, William, xi, 3
Clemens, Samuel Langhorne, 107
Clermont, 107
Clifton, Dan "Dynamite Dick", 21
Cody, "Buffalo Bill", xii
Cody, William Frederick, 62, 118
Coffeyville, Kansas, 20, 123, 124, 125, 126, 155

175

Coffman, Cleve, 156
Connelly, Charles T., 126
Crocket, Davy, 5
Cromwell, Oklahoma, 24, 26
Crook, George, 61, 118
Cubine, George, 126
Custer, George Armstrong, 6, 81, 83, 84, 117, 118

D

Dalton, Bill, 21, 123
Dalton, Bob, 20, 123, 124
Dalton, Emmett, 20, 123, 124, 126, 127
Dalton, Grat, 20, 123, 124
Daniels, Edwin B., 33, 35, 38
Daugherty, Roy "Arkansas Tom", 21, 127, 158
Denver, Colorado, 141
Dodge City, Kansas, 19, 20, 62, 71, 73
Dodge, Richard I., 19
Doniphan, Alexander W., 3
Doolin, Bill, 20, 21, 23, 24, 26, 123
Dublin, Ireland, 141
Duluth, Daniel Greysolon, 131, 133, 136
Duluth, Minnesota, 131
Dunigan, Catharine, 2

E

Earp, Wyatt Berry Stapp, 19, 69, 70, 71, 72, 74, 76
El Paso, Texas, 148
Eureka Springs, Ark., 24, 26

F

Far West, 117
Fink, Mike, 110
Fitch, John, 105, 107
Forrest, Nathan Bedford, 147
Fort Abraham Lincoln, 85
Fort Bellefontaine, Missouri, 3
Fort Bridger, Wyoming, 61
Fort Cobb, Oklahoma, 81
Fort Crawford, Wisconsin, 3
Fort Davidson, Missouri, 32
Fort Dodge, Kansas, 19
Fort Laramie, Wyoming, 61
Fort Leavenworth, Kansas, 3
Fort Lyon, Colorado, 80
Fort Smith, Arkansas, 21, 45, 48, 122
Fort Snelling, Minnesota, 133, 136
Fort Sumner, New Mexico, 139, 141
Franklin, Missouri, 90
Fulton, Robert, 107

G

Gads Hill, Missouri, 31, 38
Garcia, Manuel, 11
Garrett, Patrick ("Pat"), x
Geronimo, Chief, 4
Goodnight, Charles, 139, 141, 142
Gould, Emerson W., 108
Grant, Ulysses S., 21, 44
Grasseilliers, Medard, 131, 136
Gritty, Mike, 110
Grounds, Bob, 21

Guthrie, Oklahoma, 24

H

Hamilton, Alexander, 85
Hamilton, Lewis M., 85
Hardin, John Wesley, 145, 147, 148
Harrison, Arkansas,
Harrison *Times*, 155, 156, 157
Harrisonville, Missouri, 121
Hartnett, John, 101
Hazen, William B., 81
Hembree, M.V., 23
Henderson, Billy, 12
Hickok, "Wild Bill", 62, 63, 67, 148
Holliday, John Henry ("Doc"), 71, 73, 74, 76
Hollywood, California, 127

I

J

James, Jesse, 44
Jane, Martha "Calamity", 59, 60, 61, 62, 63, 64
Jefferson Barracks (Missouri), 3
Jefferson City, Missouri, 97
Joplin, Missouri, 158
July, Jim, 47

K

Kansas City, Missouri, 102, 121, 127

Kearny, Stephen Watts, 3, 4
Kennett, Ferdinand, 101
Kirker, James, 1, 2, 3, 4

L

Lamar, Missouri, 69, 71, 72, 76
Lee, Robert E., 21
Lewis, Meriwether, xi
Lexington *Journal*, 113
Lexington, Missouri, 111, 112, 113
Lincoln, Abraham, 31, 134
Little Rock, Arkansas, 32
Longabaugh, Harry, xi
Los Angeles, California, 11
Louisiana, 115
Love, Harry, 11, 12, 14
Loving, Oliver, 139, 141
Lull, Louis J., 32, 33, 34, 38

M

Madsen, Chris, 25
"Manifest Destiny", 1, 4, 17, 79, 85, 89
Mankato, Minnesota, 134, 136
Marshal, James Wilson, 9
Marsh, Grant Prince, 117, 118
Masterson, Bartholomew ("Bat"), 19, 26
Mather, Dave, 19, 20
McCall, Jack, 62
McCarty, William Henry, ix
McCulley, Johnson, 13
McLaury, Frank, 74
McLaury, Tom, 73

Melton, Simpson, 23
Memphis, Tennessee, 116
Monegaw Springs, Missouri, 32
Moses, Phoebe Ann, xii
Murietta, Joaquin, 9, 10, 11, 12, 14
Myers, William J., 156

N

Natchez, Mississippi, 110
Neosho *Times*, 22, 23
Newark, New Jersey, 3
Newcomb, George "Bitter Creek", 21
New Orleans, Louisiana, 108
Northfield, Minnesota, 124

O

Oakley, Annie, xii
O.K. Corral, 74, 75
Ollinger, Robert W., x
Osage Trail, 51, 55
Osceola, Missouri, 33, 35, 38
O'Sullivan, Thomas S., 99, 101

P

Parker, Isaac C., 21, 44, 46, 123
Pierce, Charley, 21, 123
Pilot Knob, Missouri, 32
Pinkerton, Allan, 31, 38
Pittsburg, Pennsylvania, 117
Portland, Oregon, xi
Porum, Oklahoma, 44, 47
Prater, Dick, 23

Princeton, Missouri, 59, 63
Pullman, George M., 95

Q

Quantrill, William Clarke, 43

R

Radisson, Pierre Esprit, 131
Raidler, Bill, 21
Reed, James C., 43, 44
Rich Hill, Missouri, 44
Rio Grande, 4
Rocheport, Missouri, 110
Roscoe, Missouri, 29, 30, 32, 35, 37, 38

S

Salem, Massachusetts, 1, 53
Saluda, 110, 111, 114
San Francisco, California, 4, 9, 12
Santa Fe, New Mexico, 4
Santa Fe Trail, 2, 4, 19, 90
Saunders, L.B., 24
Shirley, Myra Maybelle, 41
Shreve, Henry Miller, 107, 108, 114, 116
Silver City, New Mexico, ix
Sitting Bull, Chief, 6
Sonora, Mexico, 9
Southerland, Urilla, 70, 71, 76
Southwest City, Missouri, 21, 23
Starr, Belle, 42, 43, 44, 46, 47

Starr, Henry, 127, 153, 155, 156, 157, 158
Starr, Rosie Lee ("Pearl"), 43, 47, 48
Starr, Sam, 44, 46
Stinking Springs, x
St. Louis *Daily Missouri Democrat*, 96, 97, 98
St. Louis, Missouri, xi, 2, 3, 32, 97, 98, 102, 107, 110, 111, 115, 139
St. Paul, Minnesota, xi
Sultana, 116
Sundance Kid, xi
Sutter, Johann Augustus, 9

T

Taiban Creek, x
Tilghman, William Matthew, 17, 18, 19, 20, 21, 24, 25, 26
Titanic, 116
Thomas, Heck, 24
Tombstone, Arizona, 62, 69, 73
Travis, William B., 5
Truman, Harry S., 69
Tunstall, John H., x
Twain, Mark, 107, 118

U

V

W

Wagley, Marvin, 156
Wagner, Jack, 20

Walker, Alf, 20
Washington, 107, 108, 114
Weightman, "Red Buck", 21
Wesley, John, 145, 147, 150
West, Frank, 46
Wichita, Kansas, ix
Wright, James, 32, 33, 34, 38

X

Y

Yantis, Ole, 21
Yellow Hand, Chief, 118
Younger, Bob, 121, 124
Younger, Cole, 121, 124
Younger, Henry Washington, 121
Younger, Jim, 33, 34, 35, 121, 124
Younger, John, 33, 34, 35, 121

Z

Other Books by Rex T. Jackson

The Sultana Saga: The Titanic of the Mississippi
James B. Eads: The Civil War Ironclads and His Mississippi
A Trail of Tears: The American Indian in the Civil War
Traces of Ozarks Past: Outlaws, Icons, and Memorable Events
Monumental Tales from the Ozarks
Timeless Stories of the West: Mountaineers, Miners, and Indians
Curious and Unusual Civil War Stories
Notable Persons and Places in Missouri's History

About the Author

Rex T. Jackson's work has appeared in a number of publications, like **The Ozarks Mountaineer**, **Blue and Gray**, **Good Old Days**, **Ancient American**, **Capper's Weekly**, **Back Home**, **The Ozarks Reader**, **Route 66 Magazine** and others. He became a staff member of **The Ozarks Mountaineer** (based in the Branson, Missouri area) for several years and eventually founded **The Ozarks Reader Regional Magazine** and served as publisher and editor from 2004 through 2012.

www.ingramcontent.com/pod-product-compliance
Lightning Source LLC
Chambersburg PA
CBHW062040220426
43662CB00010B/1589